Gravity Pulls you In

Perspectives on Parenting Children on the Autism Spectrum

Edited by Kyra Anderson & Vicki Forman

Woodbine House   2010

The following selections are reproduced by permission of the authors:

"100 Percent" by Lesley Quinn. Originally published in the online journal, *Gettysburg Review.*

"And the Shoes Will Take Us There in Spite of the Circumference," from *Letter from the Lawn* (CustomWords, 2006), by Bobbi Lurie.

"Finally at Three, Two Words Put Together," from *When They Tell Me* (Finishing Line Press, 2009), by Grey Brown.

"The Family Gangsta," from *Weather Reports from the Autism Front: A Father's Memoir of His Autistic Son,* by James C. Wilson (McFarland, 2008).

"Proverbs 13:24," from *There Will Be Cats* (Finishing Line Press, 2009), by Aileen Murphy.

"You're Adopting Whom?" by Ralph James Savarese. Originally published in *The Los Angeles Times.*

Cataloging-in-Publication Data

Library of Congress Cataloging-in-Publication Data

Gravity pulls you in : perspectives on parenting children on the autism spectrum / edited by Kyra Anderson and Vicki Forman. -- 1st ed.
     p. cm.
  Includes bibliographical references.
  ISBN 978-1-60613-002-5
  1. Autistic children--Family relationships. 2. Parents of autistic children. 3. Parenting. 4. Parent and child. I. Anderson, Kyra. II. Forman, Vicki.
  RJ506.A9G69 2010
  618.92'85882--dc22

                                                                    2009047252

Table of Contents

Foreword *by John Elder Robison / v*
Preface *by Kyra Anderson / xi*

Part I: Notes from Autism's Edges
- Label Everything *by Anonymous / 3*
- Notes from Autism's Edges *by MothersVox / 5*
- Guilt, Denial, and Videotape *by Mama Mara / 11*
- Birthdays *by Kristen Spina / 23*
- Finally at Three: Two Words Put Together *by Grey Brown / 27*
- Middle Earth *by Drama Mama / 29*
- How to Talk to an Autistic Child *by Kimberly K. Farrar / 35*
- A Child Blinks *by Janet Kay / 37*
- The Real World of Autism: The Refrigerator Mother Club
  by Chantal Sicile-Kira / 43
- Watching My Son Watch Sleeping Beauty *by Anjie Kokan / 47*
- Sometimes, Never *by Susan Segal / 49*

Part II: String Theory
- String Theory *by Emily Willingham / 61*
- Evolution of a Fairy *by Carolyn Walker / 69*
- Live via Satellite: A Parenting Journey *by Mary McLaughlin / 79*
- Flood Plain *by Bruce Mills / 85*
- The Wages of Autism *by Kristina Chew / 93*

- Proverbs 13:24 *by Aileen Murphy* / 97
- No Pity *by Maggie Kast* / 99
- The Stone *by Barbara Crooker* / 115

Part III: And the Shoes Will Take Us There
- As Great As Trees *by Ann Douglas* / 119
- Other Child, Other Mother *by Cheri Brackett* / 125
- 100 Percent *by Lesley Quinn* / 135
- Navigating Autism *by Christine Stephan* / 141
- Driving Down the Road…and Growing Up with My Asperger's Child *by Susan T. Layug* / 147
- Heart-Shaped Rock *by Kyra Anderson* / 151
- You're Adopting Whom? *by Ralph James Savarese* / 157
- Oh, the Community *by Veronika Hill* / 161
- The Mother at the Swings *by Vicki Forman* / 163
- And the Shoes Will Take Us There in Spite of the Circumference *by Bobbi Lurie* / 167
- To Persevere *by Ralph Savarese* / 169
- The Visit *by Laura Shumaker* / 173
- Is There Anything Else We Should Know? *by B. E. Pinkham* / 181
- The Family Gangsta *by James Wilson* / 189

Contributors / *195*
Editors / *202*

Foreword

by John Elder Robison

HAVE YOU EVER WONDERED what it would be like to raise a kid with special needs? I have. You'd think I'd know, since I was a kid with special needs myself. I have Asperger's syndrome, a form of autism. The autism spectrum encompasses a wide range of conditions from total disability to mild eccentricity. I'm fortunate to be at the less-impaired end of the spectrum.

The one thing all of us on the spectrum have in common is some degree of social impairment. We may also have speech, coordination, learning, and health issues. Most of the kids who populate this book have some kind of autism. It may be called Asperger's, PDD-NOS, Rett's syndrome, or childhood disintegrative disorder. Whatever the flavor, it's all in the same family, and it stems from the same cause—configuration differences inside the brain.

I recognize myself in many of these stories. The kids bumble and struggle and fail, and I remember experiencing those very same things long ago. Then I read of their triumphs, and I remember my own small victories. Exceptional clarity of memory is fairly common among people on the spectrum.

After all the names I was called growing up, it's no surprise I saw myself as a misfit child. With that self image, I naturally thought anyone like me must be a misfit, too. However, I know different now. Today I realize that the autistic condition is really the human condition. Our hopes, dreams, and feelings are exactly the same as anyone else's. We just don't show our feelings in the conventional way, and we don't respond to other people's signals as expected. Yet inside, we are all the same.

It's very frustrating how much of the world is oblivious to that simple truth. In fact, my own distress over that bit of ignorance is one of the things that drives me to be a writer, speaker, and advocate today.

I thought I could contribute a story from the special needs child's perspective, but as I read what others had written I saw my own experience was fundamentally different. It's true I am a person with Asperger's, and I have been this way all my life, but there is a very important distinction. When I was a child, I didn't know I was autistic, and neither did anyone else. I was a just a regular kid with a lot of problems and very few friends. I was also a kid who did strange things. And I was a kid who got into a lot of trouble.

You might also think I'd understand the special-needs perspective because I raised a kid with special needs thirty-some years later. My son Cubby, who is now full-grown, also has Asperger's. However, I didn't know he was Aspergian until he was seventeen, and by then, the kid-raising was mostly done.

My special-needs parent experience was limited to watching Cubby get tested, listening to inconclusive results, and arguing with an uncooperative school system. Eventually, I gave up. "He's just not applying himself," they said. That was the same line they fed me, thirty-some years earlier, and I gave up then too. At one level I knew they were wrong, but I did not know exactly how to counter them. Naively, I believed they had my son's best interests at heart. I don't know why I should have thought that, because I knew they were not on my side as a kid, but there you have it. Maybe it's the eternal optimist in me. Anyway, I now know better. If I get a third chance, with an Aspergian grandson, I will not send him to that school system. I will make better choices.

Faced with failure and an endless hassle, I dropped out of high school, and so did Cubby. He's in college now, but he's had a harder time than he might have, had the school been a little smarter or a little more cooperative, or if I'd pushed them a lot harder. But it's not my nature to whine about such things. Cubby is in school and working two jobs, and he's making his way. That's all any of us can hope for, short of rigging a lottery machine and getting away with it.

I guess my experiences show that it was possible to raise a special-needs kid in ignorance in the sixties, and it's still possible to do it today. But can parents do a better job with the benefit of additional knowledge? My sense is, they can. That's why books like this exist. I wish I'd read one myself, long ago.

I also wish someone had told me about Asperger's when I was a teenager. I knew I had problems, and in the absence of an explanation like autism, I assumed I was just defective. The corrosive aftereffects of that childhood assumption followed me right into middle age, when I finally received a proper diagnosis. Much suffering could have been avoided if I'd known at fifteen.

That's one good side to early diagnosis. Another is the benefit of early intervention. Countless medical studies have shown that kids who receive early diagnosis followed by aggressive therapy do better than kids like me, who grew up in a free-range state.

So those are two great reasons to raise kids in a state of awareness and focus. Every parent in this book does that. If I could go back in time and raise myself again, or start over with my son, I'd do the same. What parent wouldn't?

So what's the downside? I can sum it up in two words: Reduced expectations. There is a real risk that a diagnosis will place limits on a kid's development because people will forevermore say or think, *He has autism, so he can't do that*....When I grew up, no one had any knowledge of Asperger's syndrome. That meant I was held to the same standards as every other child on the street. I had to learn to get along, attend classes, and get passing grades just like everyone else. At least, that was the idea. I followed that path till tenth grade, and then I dropped out and went my own way.

There was absolutely nothing to hold me back except myself. In fact, I often had more incentive to make my own way because I was always on the edge of starvation and ruin. In my early adult years, I lived as an outlaw, working with traveling music groups, riding with bikers, and even living in the woods. I did those things because I failed in my efforts to follow the conventional path. I dropped out of school because I could not learn in the manner the teachers taught. I could not attend college because I lacked a high school diploma. And I couldn't get a good job because I wasn't a college graduate.

But I didn't let that stop me. I made my own way and found some measure of success. However, the fact that I was an outlaw and an outsider always weighed heavily on me. I was always peeking over the sills to look at legitimate life, wondering what it might be like inside. As successful as I became, that remained the hard truth.

That's where things stood when I finally got The Diagnosis.

By the time Asperger's officially entered my life, I was forty years old. I had married and fathered a child. I had designed video games at Milton Bradley, directed research at Simplex, and then left the corporate life to found J E Robison Service Co., a specialty automobile business. Chicopee Savings Bank had named me to their board, and I was involved in my community. By most standards, I had a full life. If you asked me who I was, I'd have defined myself by those achievements.

If you asked for more, I might have fallen back on the basics. I was a white male, six foot three, two hundred twenty five pounds. Born in Athens, Georgia. If you pressed me some more, I'd volunteer that I was middle class, and generally conservative. That was how I'd describe myself.

Suddenly, with the receipt of The Diagnosis, none of that mattered. The whole concept of "people like me," took on a whole new meaning. All those former adjectives were out the window; rendered meaningless. From D-Day forward, I was a guy with Asperger's. Everything else was rendered secondary to that new facet of me.

The doctors are quick to tell you autism isn't lethal. Yet it's still one of the big scary words in medicine, like AIDS or cancer or Alzheimer's. As such, it's no surprise it came to dominate my thinking. I thought of what I'd previously known—or thought I'd known about autism. I thought of Tommy, the kid on the *St. Elsewhere* television show. I thought of *Rain Man*. I thought of all the silent lost people on the grounds of the Belchertown State School. Were they autistic, too?

Alzheimer's doesn't kill you, but it gradually takes away your mind. Would autism do that to me? Luckily, my reading abilities were still good. Nothing had started failing. Yet. I set out to learn as much as I could, while I could still read and speak.

I was in a state of extreme anxiety at first. My new diagnosis left me feeling as if I had just caught a new and deadly disease. I soon learned that wasn't the case. My midlife diagnosis was attributable to new medical knowledge, not my own deterioration. I was relieved to learn that I am actually getting slowly and steadily "better" through a lifelong process of learned adaptation and acquired wisdom.

So many things suddenly made sense. For the first time, I understood how I could be smart and yet get straight Fs in school. I saw how Asperger's had made school hard for me, and I'd done some pretty unusual stuff after dropping out. New insight brought those memories into focus, and I saw how the differences in my brain had shaped the course of my life in countless subtle ways. Yet I also realized the success I enjoyed as an adult was real, and it wasn't going away. In fact, as I moved forward with new knowledge and confidence, I saw my life was getting better every day.

Asperger's is not a disease. It's a way of being that comes from nonstandard wiring in the brain. The latest science suggests we're born different, or else we become Aspergian early in infancy. That means Aspergian life is the only life we've ever known; we don't get sick and get Asperger's as teenagers. We will always be aliens when we gaze at people who don't have Asperger's, and they will always struggle to understand our thinking.

How does that affect the parents? I never really considered that question until quite recently. This book contains many stories that describe the joy, pain, confusion, frustration, and triumph of raising a kid like me. I had no idea. It also contains stories of resolve and determination that surprise even me. Some of these people are what you might call High Performance Parents.

One thing strikes me in almost every story. Autism has taken over the lives of these people, perhaps to a greater degree than it took over my own life. I talk about life as an autistic outsider, gazing in at the world of normal people. Autism has made these parents outsiders, gazing into the unreadable minds of their own children. What a strange reversal.

When you're a kid on the spectrum, autism is all you know; all you ever knew. There was frustration at things I couldn't do, and even rage. But there was no sense of loss, because I never possessed what autism is said to have "taken away" from me. I started with a certain set of abilities and I built on them. Sure, I may have had less ability in some areas than other kids, and it sometimes hurt to realize that, but I believe we all make the most of what we have. What else could I do?

The situation for aware parents is very different. They see and imagine all manner of things their disabled kids (us) are lacking, and they suffer terribly for us. At least, that's the impression I get from talking to parents today. Was my own mother that way? I really don't know. Oblivion to others is, after all, an Asperger trait. I know I wasn't that way raising Cubby. In that sense, ignorance is indeed bliss.

But does this awareness, focus, and worry produce a better kid? Or does it just produce a more stressed parent? I really don't know. That is one of the great mysteries of kid-raising. Any of us—if aware—would do all the things parents in this book do. And the evidence in favor of early and aggressive intervention is strong. But it's a hard road, no matter how you do it.

Anyway, let's get on with the stories. I hope you enjoy them. Woof.

John Elder Robison
September 2009

Preface

by Kyra Anderson

WHEN I FIRST DISCOVERED my son had Asperger's syndrome, I felt as if I had been plucked from my orbit and flung into the birth of a new solar system, a place of swirling matter thick with energy and possibility but also utterly chaotic and frightening.

I didn't know anything about Asperger's. I didn't know anyone with autism. My closest point of reference was Dustin Hoffman's portrayal of an autistic man in the 1988 movie *Rain Man*. Most of the details in the film had faded but what stayed with me were the photographs shown during the closing credits, snapshots taken by the title character from the open top of a speeding convertible: bridge support trusses, painted lines on the highway, signs captured at odd angles—things from his point of view.

As a parent, I'll never be able to see from my child's point of view, though my son, now eight and the proud owner of his own digital camera, has amassed a collection of snapshots pitched at curious angles.

After his diagnosis at age four, the divide between my life and that of my friends grew wider as they sailed past in their minivans on the way to playgroups and schools and grocery stores and weekends away without their children. I didn't relate to their lives and they didn't seem to understand mine. They either blanched at the word autism or blinked in the face of it, looking at my son who certainly didn't fit the stereotype in their minds of a "lost and silent" child lining up train cars in the corner.

Because I could not make sense of this world to my friends, I started writing about it for myself. I found a community of blogs by parents of children on the spectrum. I felt a kinship with them. But I also felt sideswiped by the debate swirling in the autism discussion forums that very often pits parents of autistic children against autism activists.

The politics of autism can be explosive. There are many different views on autism, beginning with whether or not *autism* and *treatment* are two words that belong in the same sentence. To greatly over-simplify one debate: some parents see autism as something their child *has* and seek ways to get rid of it. Autistic activists see autism as a fundamental part of *who they are* and ask for acceptance and adaptations. This difference may explain why some parents say their child *has* autism while others say their child *is* autistic.

I wondered about the in-between. I wondered about a place where it's a given that parents embrace their autistic children, but, like all parents, they struggle to guide, challenge, and teach. I wondered about a place where acknowledging that raising a child with more than the ordinary medical, emotional, and educational needs is tricky, that this further complicates the question at the very heart of parenting: what does my child need and how can I provide this without losing my own connection to that which grounds and sustains me?

A diagnosis of autism was once a life sentence. These children were institutionalized, diagnosed as mentally ill, schizophrenic, considered victims of Bettelheim's "refrigerator mothers." The news of autism is still reported to parents and the public as devastating, a tragedy. While I am not here to discount the very real struggles and challenges faced by some children with autism and their families, the image of the autistic child as unreachable, silent, caught in a prison of repetitive behaviors is not one I recognize. Neither are images of the parent as either feverishly scraping the autism out of her child or serenely offering up platitudes about life's roses among the thorns of hardship.

These are our children. They enlighten us, delight us, annoy us, and open our hearts to injustice, outrage, exquisite beauty, and possibility. We hope to shepherd them to lives bigger and more realized than our own. When that can't happen, we grieve, we accept, we write, and through that process, we hold on to what we cannot see that may still be on the way.

Since the day I learned my son had autism, when I was tossed into this newly forming universe, when I surfed the web until the wee hours of the morning looking for answers and insight, a number of books by parents of those with special needs have been published. Aside from the rare stories of recovery and "cure," these essays typically fall into the three-fold journey of: discovery/diagnosis, fear/ grief, acceptance/lessons learned. While these offer solace to many families who recognize the process in their own lives, we need stories that look within this pattern to a deeper connection among parents, to one that broadens the view and dismantles the fear.

Is it true, as Roy Richard Grinker posits in *Unstrange Minds: Remapping the World of Autism (2007),* that there is no epidemic? That what we now have is a classification for a collection of behaviors, learning styles, and personality traits that have always been a part of the natural expression of human variation since the beginning of time?

Maybe. We don't know. But we do know more of our children are getting this diagnosis, approximately one in every 100 born by the last count. One percent. Every day, 11,000 children are born in the United States alone. That would mean that over 1,000 of them will be diagnosed on the autism spectrum.

Parenting has taken on a new dimension. We are parenting these 1,000 children, these 10,000 children, these 100,000 children. We are part of this broader conversation. We may sometimes feel as if we are in a separate solar system but we are really right here on this same round rock, under the wispy blanket of gas and dust that shows the stars only in the darkness that comes with sleep, when our minds can't tell the difference between what's real and what's imagined.

Autism acceptance and understanding is not an intellectual exercise in inclusion and the politics of acceptance and diversity. It's an everyday practical matter of learning, asking, growing, and stepping out, of being "aut," a term coined by contributor, Kristina Chew.

When my son was five years old he asked me, "How fast is the earth spinning? How fast is it spinning through space? Not around the sun, but around itself?" At the time, I was stymied, as I often am when presented with his questions. I allowed that it must be going pretty fast. In my cartoon imaginings, I saw us sticking out sideways or hanging upside down like St. Exupery's Little Prince, and I wondered, *how* does gravity *do* it and why *don't* we fall off like pennies from an upturned hand?

"Gravity, Mom," he answered for us both. And then he thought for a while. "I have an idea! Gravity doesn't really pull you *down*, it pulls you *in*. So, if you were upside down, it wouldn't pull you away from the earth, it would pull you in, toward the earth, toward its center!"

Huh. Gravity pulls you *in*.

He's right. It does pull you in, not just to the center of the earth but to the center of yourself, if you let it. Things that are weighty, things that demand a closer look, a new approach, a shift in perspective, those things pull you in. Even when you are spinning, even when you are moving much more quickly than you thought was possible, even when you find yourself in territory where instincts alone don't feel like enough to complete the revolution.

The circumference of the earth at the equator is about 25,000 miles. Every twenty-four hours, the earth travels 25,000 miles around itself through space. That means we're going more than 1,000 miles per hour. That's fast.

And we're not falling off.

PART I
Notes From Autism's Edges

Label Everything

by Anonymous

Label everything
Clothing, backpack, diapers, wipes
blankie which is contraband
but will probably be essential
on the bus, forms and permissions,
extra socks, extra sweater,
snow boots, mittens, clips,
my boy, label my boy,
my beautiful long-lashed, reading,
writing, 3-year-old, sometimes
screamy angel:
Autistic.

Notes from Autism's Edges

by MothersVox

WHEN WE FIRST ARRIVED at autism's edges, some eight years ago nearly to the day, we had no idea of the terrain we were about to enter. The contours of the landscape were obscured by well-meaning professionals who would tell us that it was simply too early to know if there was anything seriously amiss with our sweet little one who was acquiring very little language, seemed disinterested in the affairs of her peers, and who could sustain a tantrum for upwards of two hours. The well-meaning professionals did not offer us the visa of a straightforward diagnosis—something we could use to validate our entry into the world of developmental delays, differences, or disabilities. Instead, they said, your daughter's language is impaired and her play is perseverative and you ought to find a speech therapist. Without the dramatic turn of an autism diagnosis we did not so much launch into a journey as meander at the edges, at the borders, at the outskirts of a terrain that has now grown so familiar that we have come to call it home.

One of the first discoveries we made in this terrain is that things are not always what they appear to be, and, in fact, things are often quite the reverse of what one might expect. Most cultures have times or places of reversal or inversion—mirror worlds where for a day or a week and sometimes even as long as a month the world is upside down. At such times the king serves the peasant, clergy are wicked, and harlots deemed sacred, the top is replaced by the bottom. Alice is in Wonderland. Gulliver is trapped among the Houyhnhnms and

Yahoos. And everything is exactly what it usually isn't. How was I to know that autism's edges, where I would come to reside with my dear little one, would be such a place?

One of the first signs of the upside-down, oppositeville characteristics of this new terrain emerged in an early conversation with a speech-language pathologist. As you most likely already know, one of the language "defects" observed in children on the spectrum is difficulty in understanding personal pronouns. This phenomenon is attributed by autism experts such as Simon Baron-Cohen to the individual's supposed defects in theory of mind, or their "mind-blindness."

And, when you think about it, personal pronouns are fairly complicated, requiring as they do that one be able to switch back and forth rapidly between designations of "me" and "you," "mine" and "yours."

By way of example, let's say that I held up a photograph of myself and said: "It's a picture of me." If you were to respond by saying "It's a picture of me," you'd be wrong—unless, of course, you and I were both in the picture. Getting one's child to learn that "you" and "I" and "me" and "ours" are relative words is one of the early speech-language challenges.

One day, not long after our Sweet M was first evaluated for her speech and language deficits, I brought home a package of snapshots. M was about three years old at the time and she was thrilled by snapshots. She still is, though we're mostly digital in our photographs these days. As we went through the glossy prints, I spoke with Sweet M about each of them.

We came to a snapshot of me, sitting at my desk in my office.

I said, "Look M, it's me at my office."

"Me at office," she said.

"No honey, it's me—Mama—at the office," I said, pointing at myself, hearing in her reply the echolalia that the speech-language pathologist had told me to avoid reinforcing.

"No, no," she said, "Me at office."

"Honey, look, it's Mama, me, at office," I tried to persuade her.

"Me-me at office!" she said, growing increasingly adamant, though not yet frustrated enough to burst into a tantrum.

I was about to give up and move on to the next picture, when Sweet M pulled the picture away from me, and pointed to a tiny, tiny image inside the image. In the background of the photograph was a shelf in my office. On the shelf there was a framed snapshot of her. "Me—me—in picture," she said, with evident satisfaction.

She had zoomed in on the photograph inside the photograph, to the picture of herself on the shelf in my office. There was no echolalia here, just a visual acuity that defied my own imagination of the possible. She had seen an image of herself that was no more than 1 or 2 millimeters wide hidden inside a snapshot like some kind of inadvertent I Spy puzzle.

Since Sweet M had been diagnosed as "echolalic," I was on the lookout for that deficit, for evidence of her echolalia, rather than signs of her extraordinary visual intelligence.

A few days later I was on the phone with the speech-language pathologist who had done Sweet M's evaluation. I was delighted to share my error with her—to tell her how at first I'd thought that M was having a problem with pronoun confusion, but that actually I just wasn't seeing what she was seeing, and therefore wasn't understanding that she was right, that she was in the picture. I was very excited and effusive telling the speech-language pathologist about my discovery.

"Yes," she said, her voice flat and deflating, "M has splinter skills."

"Splinter skills?" I asked, stunned by the sound of this language.

"Yes, splinter skills. She has some specific strengths. That's typical of kids like M."

I was rendered as speechless as my child. A splinter skill? In the world of the neurotypical, most people are allowed to understand that their personal characteristics may be viewed as assets or liabilities, depending on the context. The ability to focus and persevere is tenacity in one setting, obsessiveness or perseveration in another. But in the land of developmental diagnostics—at least among the clinicians we first encountered—there were only liabilities. Everything was to be converted into evidence of the four D's: damaged, defective, diseased, disabled. We might also call this Autism Axiom #1: What's bad about my kid is bad, and what's good about my kid is also bad.

Writing in 1943, psychiatrist Leo Kanner called the skills of autistic kids "islets of ability." I'm not sure who came up with the even more dismissive term "splinter skills." It sounds as though we ought to be looking for a pair of tweezers to yank those skills right out of them. The earliest example of this language of "splinter skills" that I've come across is in a 1971 article by M.K. De Myer et al., in the first issue of the *Journal of Autism and Childhood Schizophrenia*. But that was the first issue of this publication, so who knows—clinicians might have been using the splinter skill language for much longer.

Personally, I prefer Kanner's "islets of ability." Sounds rather nice…though I can't figure out if I should be imagining small, lush, tropical islands of skill in a great sea of plentitude, or great craggy stones jutting up from an ocean of ineptitude.

In the landscape at autism's edges, when you cross over into the land of pathology, everything is necessarily pathological. By falling into this customary way of thinking—by looking for the pathology instead of the person—I had rendered myself temporarily mind-blind to Sweet M's realities and to her capacities.

But when what is good is bad, it is not long before other reversals take shape, and what is bad can become almost good. Not long ago, my own worst parenting moment became evidence of Sweet M's great progress. One evening, stricken with a paralyzing migraine, I reverted to a parody of bad parenting. Sweet M, now ten years old and reasonably fluent in English, was quarrelling with her father about bath time. I was curled up in a fetal position on the bed, hoping that the migraine dry heaves would not resume and praying that someone would just come in and shoot me in the head to put me out of my misery.

It was time for her bath, but her father had made the tactical error of insisting that she go to her bath in the middle of a TV program she was watching, rather than waiting for the end of it and then sending her off to the tub.

So Sweet M came in whining to me. "Mommmmm, Mommmmm, Dad turned off my show. Help me. It's not fair."*

Grunt from me.

---

* In point of fact Sweet M does not call us Mom and Dad, but rather by our first names. To avoid using names or initials, I'm reverting to the typical nomenclature of parenting.

"Mommmm, Mommmm, come on and talk to him, you have to talk to him."

"I'm sick, you guys figure it out," I muttered back.

"But...but...but...it's my show . . ." she continued, her voice louder and more excruciating with those distinctive whining tones against my throbbing head.

I marshalled my last ounce of coherence and energy, lugged myself into the living room, restored her show, and said in my most deranged parent voice: "There. Your show is on. Watch it. When it's over, take your bath. And I don't want to hear another word from you, young lady."

She regarded me with amused amazement, nodded solemnly and said, "O-key-doe-key."

And then I realized what I'd said—something I'd never said in all the years I'd been parenting her—I told her to stop talking. And I can. Because now she talks.

Hallelujah—I can be just as bad a parent as the next parent and she'll survive. I never thought I'd be proud of my worst moment.

But therein lies the secret power of autism—what's bad is bad, what's good is bad, and now, farther into the journey, even what's bad can be good.

Guilt, Denial, and Videotape

by Mama Mara

WHEN MY KIDS WERE little, I had a nasty little habit. I knew I was doing a bad thing. "It isn't healthy," I told myself. "I'm going to regret it later." But it was like an addiction, and I simply couldn't stop myself.

Time and time again, I inserted The Video and pressed play.

The sound of my nasal, bubbly voice always made me wince. It was my home-movie voice, self-consciously narrating my precious baby's every move. Even more annoying was my poor control of the camera. The image on the TV screen often bounced and blurred, only intermittently focusing on my son's intense face, his cheeks a sun-kissed fuchsia, his chin wet and shiny with its ubiquitous supply of drool.

The Video went something like this:

"Rocky! How old are you?" I ask. He doesn't answer. He is too busy playing with his favorite "toy," an olive-green, Wisconsin Bell touch-tone telephone that hasn't worked since 1988.

"Hello!" he yells excitedly into the receiver, as if he's been waiting for an important call all day. Then he quickly hangs up, his goodbye directed not at an imaginary caller but at the receiver that he's slammed down into its cradle. He pauses and then quick-draws the phone back to his ear. "Hello!" Hang up. "Goodbye."

"Rocky, you're eighteen months old." Still he ignores me. The game continues uninterrupted until he misjudges the size of the unwieldy receiver and smacks himself hard in the center of his forehead during a particularly energetic "hello." Rebuffing any comfort, he ignores me as a tear trembles on his eyelashes and a giant lump rises near his temple.

"Hello!" Hang up. "Goodbye." "Hello!" Hang up. "Goodbye." "Hello!" Hang up. "Goodbye." "Hello!" Hang up. "Goodbye." "Hello!" Hang up. "Goodbye." "Hello!" Hang up. "Goodbye." "Hello!" Hang up. "Goodbye." "Hello!" Hang up. "Goodbye." "Hello!" Hang up. "Goodbye." "Hello!" Hang up. "Goodbye." "Hello!" Hang up. "Goodbye."

Just weeks after I taped The Video, Rocky started to have trouble talking. At first, words seemed to get stuck in his mouth. "Hello! Gggggggg–. Gggggggggggggggggg–. Hello, ggggoodbye," he'd finally blurt out, his face red with exertion.

Before long, he stopped talking altogether. His pediatrician sent us to an otolaryngologist for a complete evaluation. After a series of tests, she invited me into her office, which appeared to be little more than a storage room with a desk. Boxes, files, toys, and medical equipment were crammed so tightly into the space that we were forced to sit with our knees touching. Rocky amused himself by lining up magic markers on the dirty floor between our feet.

The woman inhaled deeply, pasted a grim look on her face, and said, "I have to tell you something that's going to be very hard to hear, and you need to take it very seriously."

She went on to describe my beautiful, intelligent, perfect son in nightmarish jargon. Eye gaze avoidance. Ritualized touching of toys. Low muscle tone. Fine and gross motor delays, speech dysfluency, echolalia. Pervasive developmental delay.

I did what any mother in love with her child would do. I ignored her.

Well, okay, not really. I got a second opinion. A well-regarded professional confirmed my belief that the oto-whatdyacallit was a crazy mean lady. (I'm paraphrasing, of course; the professional used impressive, multisyllabic words to denigrate her peer.) She assured me that Rocky just needed speech therapy. Soon this little bump in Rocky's developmental path would be a distant memory.

I patted myself on the back for not overreacting and found a wonderful speech therapist. She was a petite, grandmotherly woman with the bedside manner of an angel. She worked with Rocky for eighteen months, watching his age and size double while his developmental problems increased exponentially. It was late summer when she took my hand and gently broke my heart.

"I'm no expert, but I'm noticing little things," she said. Ironically, she was unable to look me in the eye as she told me, "He doesn't maintain eye contact. His play isn't really typical for his age. He relies an awful lot on memorized passages instead of spontaneous speech. It's probably a good idea to have him checked out by a specialist."

Tearfully, I contacted a screening service through our school district. A few weeks later, the district's developmental specialist team made a house call and said four simple words that changed our lives.

"Your son has autism."

"Hello!" Hang up. "Goodbye." "Hello!" Hang up. "Goodbye."

In the months after the diagnosis, I watched The Video with obsessive fervor. I would scream at the TV monitor at my naïve former self. "Open your eyes, you idiot! Don't you see it? God, why don't you see it?"

I could see it in hindsight, of course. The Video documented my son's first "perseverative interest in a peculiar non-toy object," a classic behavior of autistic children.

For two years, Rocky was obsessed with telephones. Pay telephones were particularly enticing. It was impossible to pass a bank of them without allowing him several minutes to ritualistically touch each one. He once threw a loud, humiliating, thirty-minute tantrum when I told him he couldn't touch all the flashing buttons on the nice bank lady's multi-line reception phone. And he carried his olive-green Wisconsin Bell model around everywhere, the way most kids might carry a beloved teddy bear.

If only I'd understood back then that Rocky's phone worship was a screaming billboard advertising his autism. If only I'd listened to the crazy mean lady. All those months of early intervention were lost because I *didn't listen*. I blew it.

This was the ugliest aspect of my nasty little habit: video-inspired self-flagellation.

Poor, poor Rocky, I lamented. Doomed from the day he found himself in my womb. Visions of teratogens danced through my head. Maybe his autism was caused by those anti-nausea suppositories I used to combat my debilitating morning sickness. Or the coffee I should have stopped drinking. Or maybe it was the combined effect of too little protein and too many Cheetos.

Nah. It probably didn't matter what I ingested, I concluded. My true sin was passing on my defective genes. I had no proof, of course; scientists hadn't (still haven't) yet isolated the autism marker. But I could build a strong anecdotal case. My cousin also had an autistic son. I could point to countless relatives, undiagnosed, perhaps, but clearly socially-awkward, sensory-defensive, and undeniably weird.

Heck, sometimes I could convince myself that *I* was autistic. I don't always feel comfortable looking people in the eye. I'm clumsy. And I swear I can hear the high-pitched hum that emanates from fluorescent lighting. How unforgivably arrogant I was to procreate, I chastised myself at these moments. I should have had a scarlet "*A*" branded on my forehead at the wedding ceremony.

Then again, other times I wondered if maybe Rocky was a perfect baby when he entered the world. It was my Mother Nurture, not Mother Nature, that caused his disability. In full Video vilification mode, I would cringe at the memory of how long it took to get his first high fever under control when he was an infant. I probably fried his brain. I Ferberized him too early. I potty-trained him too late. I made him listen to Broadway show tunes and Sinead O'Connor. The kid never had a chance.

To snap out of this self-loathing riff, sometimes I tried to focus on the positive things I'd done since Rocky was diagnosed. But my mind rebelled, instead meticulously calculating the thousands of hours and dollars I'd spent on fruitless therapies.

I tried sensory integration training when Rocky was four, forcing him to wear earphones that blasted what sounded like bad European techno-music into his ears for two hours a day. While he listened to the noise, I brushed his tender skin and manipulated his joints to stimulate his "proprioceptive" sense. The result: he started to throw up after every session. I quit against therapist's advice. She actually wanted me to continue, claiming that the puking proved the therapy was having an impact. Before I walked out of her office, I briefly considered putting the headphones on Rocky right there so he could projectile-vomit all over her.

The next summer, I took him to a therapist who had him sit in front of a computer screen twice a week, clapping in time to a digital metronome. If memory serves, the goal was to "realign" his brainwaves. It sounded daffy, but I went along with it, suspending my disbelief so I could entertain a little hope. After several months, even the therapist conceded that there had been no measurable improvement. At least Rocky enjoyed the clapping (a veritable bargain at just $150 an hour).

And what about all the programs I *didn't* try? I rejected hyperbaric oxygen chamber therapy, music therapy, vision therapy, cranio-sacral therapy: none of them ventured, nothing gained. Even the wildly-popular casein/gluten-free diet got my seal of rejection. I insisted it was too much work for too little potential gain. Translation: rather than do a little extra cooking and shopping, I chose to slowly poison my son. Translation: I was Evil incarnate.

The thought of poisoning my son led me to my next wave of self-torment. I once joked that Rocky rattled when he walked because he took so many pills. (I will go to Hell for that crack alone.) He started taking psychiatric medications when he was just four years old. At that time, his anxiety was so severe that he said it felt like he had a dragon under his skin. I promised him we would slay the dragon, using pharmaceutical swords.

Psychiatrists warned me that no medication treats autism; meds can only help control the symptoms. Since Rocky had a lot of symptoms to control, I gave him a lot of drugs over the years: pills to increase his attention, reduce his compulsions, extinguish his anxiety, tame his phobias, ameliorate his depression, quell his rage, and on and on. Rattle, rattle, rattle.

With intense shame, I admitted to myself that I never truly considered the long-term effects of all this pill-popping. What if his adulthood was spent suffering from permanent dry mouth, lethargy, swollen joints, stunted growth, floppy gums, hair loss, hair growth, stomach cramps, suicidal thoughts, dystonia, and tardive dyskinesia? Not a pretty picture.

Lost in tortured thought about my son's bleak future, I was always startled by the abrupt end of The Video, the image dissolving suddenly into TV snow, Rocky's voice suddenly replaced by the deafening hiss of static. Each time I hit the eject button, I vowed it was the last time. I'd never watch *It* again.

Insert. Press play. *"Hello!" Hang up. "Goodbye."*

One time, one glorious time, I watched The Video with fresh, optimistic eyes. Suddenly, the phone game was adorable to me. *He* was adorable. He was intelligent, affectionate, silly, creative, loving, engaging, enthusiastic.

And then I had an epiphany (aka bout of temporary insanity): *Rocky's not autistic at all. All the experts are wrong.*

I was in denial, and it felt great.

With growing excitement, I actually considered saying the words all husbands dream of hearing: "You were right."

For the first year after the diagnosis was made, my husband refused to buy it. A skeptic by nature, he speculated that the so-called specialists who'd diagnosed Rocky saw autism everywhere they looked. Autism was the diagnosis du jour, and every newly-diagnosed child was worth thousands of dollars to money-hungry therapists, psychiatrists, and other charlatans. He called autism "the A-word" and treated it as an obscenity, never to be uttered in polite company.

I couldn't simply dismiss the diagnosis. Denial eluded me, so I chased it. I tried to *prove* the diagnosis was wrong. In that first year, I bought every book about autism I could get my hands on. And then, wielding a highlighter pen like a weapon, I endeavored to kill the messengers.

In predatory fashion, I hunted through dense texts until I found my targets. Example: One author noted that a child on the autism spectrum *usually fails to show basic developmental imitation, like waving bye-bye.* Aha! Rocky's first word was "bye-bye," accompanied by a wave, at age ten months. See, he's *not* autistic!

In neon pink, I highlighted every passage I could find to cast doubt on Rocky's autism-ness. After a while, all my books appeared to have contracted some sort of pox. For a short time, I really believed that I had the diagnosis beat.

But I couldn't stay in Denial long. I reread every single book and highlighted paragraphs that *supported* Rocky's autism diagnosis, this time in neon yellow. By the end of my research, my books were all suffering from severe jaundice.

I showed the diseased pages to my doubting spouse. Together, we conceded defeat in the battle against the dreaded label.

After sobering up from the intoxication of Denial, grief and despair overwhelmed me. I sank into a deep depression. Friends urged me to get help, so I reluctantly went to a support group for parents of autistic children.

The support group was small, maybe six other moms sitting in cold metal folding chairs, drinking warm apple juice, and eating generic oatmeal cookies. I sat stiffly, hoping I wouldn't burst into tears in front of these strangers.

"So, is your son verbal?" one mother asked. When I said he was a big talker, she nodded dismissively and snapped, "Lucky you."

It was obvious that, in her mind, Rocky wasn't autistic enough. For some strange reason, I felt compelled to prove her wrong.

"My son throws up if he sees white food," I proclaimed with perverse pride. "And most of his speech is delayed echolalia!"

That got a few impressed nods from the other mothers. But soon each woman topped me with bizarre tales of bloody self-injury, midnight hunts for their escaped "runners," and gut-wrenching visiting days at the local psychiatric hospital.

I ducked out of the meeting early to retrieve Rocky from the daycare room. He was busily linking up magnetic Thomas the Tank Engine locomotives to oil tanker cars, coal hoppers, and cabooses. To his left, another boy about his age was busily flapping his hands in front of his face while making wet raspberry noises. Now, *that* kid looked autistic. In comparison, my son was as "typpie" as Beaver Cleaver.

I never returned to the support group. It had done its job. My belief that I didn't belong there made me smile for the first time in weeks. I had my Denial back!

Friends and family fueled my doubts about Rocky's autism. "He seems normal enough to me," they'd say. Or "He does *that* because you *let* him. He's not autistic; he's spoiled." And my personal favorite: "My uncle did that when he was a kid, and look at him now. He's a successful and highly-respected proctologist." I began to cling to the hope that Rocky would grow out of his autism. Of course, as a seasoned worrier, I subsequently fretted that he might one day become a proctologist.

One person in particular gave me the most hope that Rocky was indeed a "normal" child. That was my second son, Taz.

I found out I was pregnant with Taz one month before Rocky was diagnosed. The developmental specialist team suggested that I seek genetic counseling, but I refused. "Too late," I had sobbed.

Unlike the quiet, introspective baby his big brother had been, Taz was full of energy, constantly cuddling, and prone to wild giggling and explosive tantrums. But as he entered his toddler years, I realized that Taz wasn't really so different from Rocky. Like his big brother, he wasn't particularly interested in toys. He loved to hear the same books over and over. He hated to get his hands dirty. Yet he was a so-called "regular" kid. Maybe Rocky wasn't autistic; I just made kids with quirky temperaments.

What really gave me hope, though, was watching Rocky's play skills flourish as he interacted with Taz. He loved to make his baby brother laugh, playing peek-a-boo until both boys were shrieking with glee. He started to make more eye contact. He exhibited some new social skills. It seemed like Taz's normalcy was contagious. I began to believe that, with enough exposure to his little brother, Rocky would be cured. Taz would be our little Miracle Worker.

That didn't happen. To the contrary, Taz began to show signs of developmental delay himself. He didn't start talking until he was two, so he had to join his brother in speech therapy. Around that time, he began to play something he called "door game," opening and shutting anything on hinges for hours on end. *Open. Shut. Open. Shut.* The constant banging noise drove me bonkers.

By the time he entered preschool, Taz was extremely rigid in his habits. He insisted on wearing the same clothes every day and refused to participate in group activities. His baffled teachers reported that he entertained himself by playing with a pirate ship, performing an intricate series of motions, and reciting the same words verbatim day after day after day.

History repeated itself. More doctors. More evaluations. Another house call by the specialists. "Taz has a Pervasive Developmental Delay." *Hello! Goodbye. Open. Shut.*

Rocky gave up his fascination with telephones years ago, but he's never stopped having perseverative interests. Through his many obsessions, I've learned so much. I know the proper names of most modern construction vehicles. I've memorized the locations of the world's tallest skyscrapers. And I can list every rock star who ever died by choking on vomit.

He's almost thirteen years old now and brimming with hormones. Currently, his all-consuming topic is DVDs. He memorizes the features of every DVD release on the market, along with the customer quality ratings he checks daily on his favorite Internet movie site. When I pick him up after school, he doesn't even greet me. He bounds into the car and says something like, "Mom, would you like me to list all of the *Planet of the Apes* movies and what special features are available on the DVDs?" When I say I need a "movie-talk" break, he recites the list to himself in a very loud whisper.

He still rattles when he walks, taking a complex pill cocktail that is currently taming the dragon under his skin. And so far, the side effects have been manageable. In fact, the only long-term side effect I can identify from his years of meds and therapy is an extreme aversion to European techno-music. He prefers classic rockers like Jimi Hendrix (who, in 1970, was the first famous rock star to die by choking on vomit).

Rocky still gags at the sight of white food at meals, but he's found ways to compensate. Each morning at his request, I tint his milk green so he can pour it onto his cereal. Now I'm the one who gags.

He often wears his autism with pride, feeling sorry for people who don't feel as passionate about his topics as he does, who can't memorize data like a computer, and who are limited by social conventions that make no sense.

Other times, he becomes desperately despondent about how different he is from his peers. "They all fool around just for fun. I don't get it," he sighs. He recently begged me to relax my rules about his use of obscenities. It's one social skill he can pull off convincingly, and he insists it makes him less of an outcast. I can't think of a better reason to have a potty mouth.

Taz is ten years old and still a bundle of exasperating energy. His journey has been much harder than Rocky's so far. He began having seizures when he was six. By age nine, he was flying into violent rages almost daily, kicking dents into my bedroom wall and bruises all over my body. It took a month-long hospitalization to stabilize him, and I've had to learn better parenting skills so I can be the kind of mother he needs. He suffers from memory loss, delusions, language aphasia, anxiety, phobias, obsessive/compulsive rituals, cognitive deficits…the list goes on and on.

But there is another list. It's a list of all the things that make me so grateful to be his mother. He has the brightest smile in the world. His imagination is incredibly vivid, allowing him to concoct wonderful stories about monsters and pirates and vanilla factories and killer crocodiles and magic princes. He has big dreams, hoping one day to dig his own gold and diamond mine, write and direct a bloody slasher film, and start a club with rhinestone-studded uniforms that he will design himself. Recently, the principal at his elementary school gave him a Good Citizen Award because he looked after a child who was injured on the playground. See? *This* list goes on and on, too.

I'm pleased to admit that I haven't compulsively watched *It—The Video*—in years. So it was a real kick recently when the boys and I found it in our pile of home movies and watched *It* together. We laughed at little Rocky's serious expression as he played the phone game, looking as if he were a businessman racing to beat a deadline. They teased me for my nasal, bubbly narration. They asked me to tell them their favorite stories about when they were babies, like the time Rocky decided to make an indoor sandbox by emptying a mega-sized container of black pepper on the floor. Or the time Taz became fascinated with the elastic on my sweatpants and pulled on it so hard that he exposed my white Wisconsin rear to a high-school boys' basketball team.

As The Video continued to play, my eyes filled with tears. I realized that for too long I had treated *It* like some sort of crime documentary, alternately seeking to prove my guilt or innocence.

Now I saw that it was just a home movie. Created with love, it sought only to give joy and receive attention, and it deserved to be treasured forever.

Just like my two beautiful boys.

Birthdays

by Kristen Spina

THE SMALL WHITE ENVELOPE slips from between the pages of *Land of Nod*, hitting the floor with a soft thump. Today's stack of mail is a familiar mix of bills, catalogs, a *Pennysaver,* and this—this tiny envelope, no bigger than a deck of cards, addressed to my five-year-old son.

Without even opening it, I know what it contains. An invitation. As I bend to pick up the envelope, I can't help but wonder if this latest invite is from a family we know or from a school friend whose parents I have not met.

Before we came to live on the outskirts of the autistic spectrum a couple of years ago, I never gave much thought to the downside of birthday parties. When I was pregnant with my son, I spent a lot of time fantasizing about our lives, and the life I imagined was certainly not the life we have. In the life I imagined, birthday parties were soft colors and laughter and bubbles floating through the air. In the life we have, birthday parties are bright and jarring and sometimes even a little scary.

Diagnosed with sensory processing disorder and pervasive development disorder-not otherwise specified, my son is easily overwhelmed and very often out of sync with his surroundings. It takes hours of coaching and role-playing on our part and every ounce of strength he has to successfully—or even somewhat successfully—navigate the fanciful parties thrown for his peers. Like any kid his age, my son thrills at the idea of a birthday party. And what's not to like? A recent invite was to an arcade, complete with bumper cars, flying helicopters, a maze, and video games. Another was to an indoor playground with an obstacle course, ball pit, freeze dancing, and a bubble machine. On more than one occasion, as I've struggled to keep my son from dissolving into a puddle on the floor, I've mourned the demise of simpler parties—a handful of kids in the backyard with cake and a few party favors.

I make a clean slice with a letter opener across the top of the envelope. I pull out the invitation and see that the party is for one of the girls in my son's class—a child I can't place and a family I don't know. Though I am tempted to toss the invitation into the trash with today's *Pennysaver*, I tack it to the bulletin board and check the calendar.

When my son was younger, I could decide whether or not we would attend without involving him. But at five years old, kids talk and secrets are not so easily kept. So now, when an invitation comes, we discuss it. We talk about the party place, the kids who might be there, the activities and games they might play, and we decide together. At least that's how I like to think about it. More often than not, I share with him all the things that worry me—the chaos, the noise, the crowd—and he assures me that he can handle it.

And much of the time he can. But very often, he can't. People who don't know my son often mistake him for a typical kid. But he is not typical. His issues are complex. At two years old, he couldn't negotiate the most basic playground equipment or hold a crayon and draw a straight line. There were other signs as well.

By the time he turned three, there was no denying we were in trouble. He cried at nursery school. He cried at home. He couldn't tolerate change of any kind. Loud noises rattled him, children overwhelmed him, and he spent his days angry, frustrated, and scared. No day was a good day.

Two years later, we have many good days. Therapy works. Time and experience help too. We're learning to adapt, to cope, and to figure things out, together and with the help of some very smart therapists and teachers. Every day is a new day. And so when a small white envelope addressed to my son lands in our mailbox, I may be tempted to toss it aside, but I don't. He's more than earned the right to try.

I am more comfortable with invites from families we know—kids my son socializes with on a fairly regular basis and their parents who have over time become familiar with our challenges. At these affairs, I even dare to attempt adult conversation and give my son some space to practice new skills, like waiting his turn and being a good sport.

With people we don't know as well, the schoolyard and play-ground acquaintances, it's a bit trickier.

For now, I put this latest invitation out of my mind. In a few days, I will call and introduce myself to the birthday girl's mom. I will have to decide how much information to share with her about my son. That particular conversation never gets any easier. I don't enjoy giving up details to strangers. I will tell this mom that because my son is still learning to negotiate social events, we would like to arrive a few minutes early so that he has a chance to settle in before the party gets started. I will tell her that I am happy to help in any way that I can—though, the truth is, I will likely have my hands full helping my son.

I never imagined that a birthday party would give rise to such complex feelings on my part. When I think about the child my son was at two and three, I am in awe of the little boy he has become. He is connecting and making friends and getting invited to partici-pate—and that's what I need to hold on to. It is what gives me my greatest hope. And so, chances are, when party day arrives, we'll don our party faces and head out the door with great expectations.

I may walk a fine line between should we or shouldn't we, but I know we should. My son will never learn to find his way unless we step out and into life. And despite my unease, he really should pin the proverbial tail on the donkey—regardless of where it lands—just like any other five-year-old.

Finally at Three: Two Words Put Together

by Grey Brown

Speaking to the blades
of our roaring attic fan,
she commands,
Off noise.
Off noise to the noise in her head
to the grating of nerves,
the sizzle of synapses not quite connecting.
Off to the static of life,
to the rip of venetian blinds
arching her month-old back above my lap.
Off to the knives of traffic noise
as we venture out
for a stroller ride.
Off to the boat whistle
that day she nearly leapt
straight from my arms.
Off and death to suction cups that scream
as the bath mat is wrenched from the tub.
Off to sinister balloons suddenly bursting,
off to dogs barking large and small

off to the pop of bubble wrap,
off to the hair dryer
off to thunder
and now, above all
off to the toilets
all the toilets
going off one after the other
in the stalls going on forever
here at the Wonderful World of Disney.

Middle Earth
by Drama Mama

THE DAY MY DAUGHTER, Miss M, was born, I was so ener-
gized I could not sleep. I did laps around the maternity ward, feeling for
the stretch-mark fall-out and manufacturing colostrum all the while. I
giddily chunked my way over to the nursery, where babies snoozed in
their burrito get-ups with cheery little announcements heralding the
latest and greatest in trendy names. I sought out my new daughter,
unbelievably blonde and alert and blinking in her tiny bassinet. I had
a very strong sensation that rattled my already pulsating uterus.

She was alone.

Certainly, she was not alone in that room full of babies, but she
was alone in her place in the world. I felt it. My eyes welled up, and I
remember thinking that it was just the hormones, but in that instant,
I knew that my daughter would make her journey on her own, in her
way, and perhaps, not necessarily with the rest of her freshman class
of newborns snoring heavily in that room.

Two and a half years later, an evaluator handed me the pamphlet
with the picture of an adorable-but-dazed-looking infant that read
Autism and Your Child. I died that day. The jovial woman who once
laughed with her head thrown back now slumped and asked God
why? The woman who stood over her sleeping child's bed, drunk
with happy anticipation of the impending day, now found it hard
to look at her damaged charge. There were to be no ballet lessons,
no senior prom, and worst, no friends. No hope. I walked in a fog

of unworthiness. My child was defective; something was wrong that had to be fixed. Rebuilt. Like the Bionic Woman, she had to be made again, this time with the *right* components: speech that was *productive*, focus that followed *a linear line*, a body that did not buzz about like a motor gone awry.

All of the things that once charmed and delighted me about my daughter now had an ugly cast of wrongness about it.

At three, Miss M taught herself to read. Really read. She read with feeling and understood the content. When I marveled to the evaluator at the time, she shrugged it off and mumbled something about HYPERLEXIA and went on about IMMEDIATE intervention BEFORE IT WAS TOO LATE.

A few years later, Miss M was enrolled in a mostly-good pre-school. She was reading picture books to the other students. I was impressed, and mentioned to the teacher that this was a great step in Miss M's social development. The teacher gave me a tight smile, and told me that one of the other parents was worried that her child was not yet reading, because she'd heard Miss M's impressive performance. "I told her that she should worry if her child *was* already reading—I mean, that's a serious red flag." I am still scratching my head over that comment.

During the many assessments in preschool, crammed into a tiny stuffy room, seated on tiny preschool chairs, dead plants on the windowsill, I'd bring up the topic of Miss M's *brain*. Her beautiful, gorgeous, huge brain. Now, I'm not one of those mothers who thinks that her daughter's challenges are because she is "gifted"—certainly not. But if I were? I wouldn't apologize for believing in my child. Besides, I do think that it is part of the puzzle. Our puzzle.

For some strange reason, it seems impossible for autistic children to have talents that are not considered "splinter skills." When my daughter writes an incredible story or poem, I don't think that it's incredible because she is autistic, it's incredible because she is incredible. In meetings, the "experts" have qualified her talents or gifts as an offshoot to her neurologic differences. When do her gifts just become her gifts? When does who she is become her personality, and not a defect?

Miss M is now in grade school. I sit through many parent-teacher conferences. Our fifteen minutes book along briskly, usually with an explanation of the report card and some sort of nod to the IEP. We quickly discuss goals and incentives, but never do we discuss the many, many things that Miss M does *right*.

And there are many, many things that she does with blinding ease and grace. Miss M reads with expression, fully and with passion. She is a remarkable actress, presumably, because "well, she's good at it because it's not her." I wonder if it could have anything to do with the fact that her mother is an actress, and that she has been exposed to the arts since infancy? She possesses empathy beyond most people's comprehension, complimenting my costumer on her hard work—"that must have taken you hours—are your fingers sore?" and demanding dollars for every homeless person that we happen to encounter. She has a keen analytical mind, and a great sense of humor—she is abstract and not at all literal-minded, as many expect her to be.

We have done our penance, as prescribed, and logged thousands of hours of therapies and interventions, poking and prodding and nodding and much stroking of beards. As far as I can tell, Miss M has remediated herself. She has remedied the situation. She goes to *regular* school, *regular* camp, and *regular* extracurricular activities. She *looks* like the average kid, has the same likes as the average kid, and bears no earmarks of autism. Not a hand flap or perseveration in sight.

But she is still alone.

We have entered the world between, a limbo between Autismland and the alarming normalcy of the Neurotypicals. She belongs to neither team, but is a being unto herself, and blessedly, she is content with her station in life. She skips out of school, past the girls in her class who wear fashionable jeans and are on the fast track to bitchy. She does not notice that she is the only child leaving not in a pair or pack but alone. No matter. She has a fantasy scenario that she wants to "think out" in the latest chapter of the novel she is writing. In her head, while sitting on the edge of her bed, her fingers walking out the character's movements, she works out her latest plot twist. She cheerily stops after a half-hour, to give her brain a "rest."

She pretends to wipe her brow. "Whew," she says, "it gets *intense* in there," and she taps at her forehead and smiles.

She knows her limits. She knows from inappropriateness. She has been impeccably, relentlessly instructed in the art of blending in.

But not too much.

Not enough to make a real friend at school. Not enough to really care that she is not invited to sleepovers and parties. She is content in the coziness of her family and close, comfortable friends, and her books. Her fantasies. Her dramatic role-plays.

Now that the rehabilitation is nearly complete, the new Bionic Girl is formed—what now? Is it too much to want her to blend in? Blend in to what? And whom? She has told me that the other kids, "just aren't very interesting," and who am I to disagree? I cringe from time to time, her awkwardness like a beacon to me.

And yet.

We are well into our journey out of Autismland. You might say that the ski rack is still firmly on the roof rack, but we're ready to unpack our bags as we settle into our new home. We are always ready, waiting, watching. How do we settle back into family hood as we pat down our bodies after the shock of Developmental Correctional Institution? I imagine it's a little like a convict emerging from prison, blinking into the sunshine, wondering what to do with herself as she arrives home, the house smaller than she remembered, with a flower bed sorely in need of maintenance, and peeling paint chips waving in the breeze.

There is nothing to do but resume, work, acknowledge, facilitate, but realize that there is the matter of your life, and there is plenty to be weeded and watered and tended to. So slowly, I find things that bring me joy that have nothing to do with autism.

That is hard to do.

Try to spend a day without mentioning the word *autism*, much less *thinking* about autism.

So it becomes a part of the everyday vernacular, as easy as saying the word hello, or telephone, or door.

The more frequently the word is used, the less potent its meaning. The autism becomes meaningless. I can take classes, throw myself into work, go out with friends and shrug the autism off like a pair of slippers. The more that I normalize my life, find interests and passions that feed my soul, the less significant are the hurtful statements, the quizzical looks, the school bullshit in general.

A thousand years ago, I was an actress of some renown, who led a full and exciting life that many probably cannot fathom—jumping planes, traveling on a moment's notice, bowing before a howling, gurgling crowd, drinking in whatever it was that I happened to be serving that evening.

That life did not include a special needs child, or responsibility other than selecting what stinky cheese I would buy on the way home from rehearsal that day. My world revolved around profitable creativity—a hired gun of imagination and entertainment.

In dramatic theory, the great Constantin Stanislavski poses the "What if" as a departure point in order to free actors, to unbind them from any preconceived ideas or assumptions about their character. In my years as an actor, it was the question that unlocked doors, unleashed blocked memories, provided limitless potential.

As an actor, the potential for using *What If* is limitless. I can *what if* myself into infinity if I wish. No matter how silly the presumption, my most truly present actor-self can explore and discover a myriad of character choices and plot twists formerly unseen or even unthought by the playwright.

And so. What. If. This. Is. It.

What if this is the most that my child will develop? What then? Is it freeing to let go of any preconceptions? Does it crush me? Does it diminish her worth? Mine? What if my child was neurotypical tomorrow, not a trace of autism anywhere? Does it change my life? How so? What does that look like? Smell like? Does it change the way I feel about her?

What if autism, in its infuriating mystery, has also opened our eyes to possibilities without limits? We have hiked up a very steep mountain and are still standing, legs shaking, at the top. Why not go for one more?

I opt to use the *What If* in a positive vein, as if her potential is as endlessly wide and open as the mystery surrounding her. Certainly, she has surprised me at every turn, from her initial diagnosis to her phenomenal recovery and residual uniqueness.

Or better yet, What about *Why Not? Why Not* to autism, to sameness and different-ness? My daughter wishes to play alone at times? *Why not?* She wishes to engage in a political debate whilst her peers look askance at the girl-no-one-knows-what-to-make-of? *Why the hell not?* We've done all the "remediation" that we can do, and what's left is a soul as innocent and creative and wonderful as it's going to be.

Okay. Okay then. I open my arms wide and position my legs in a wide stance and say *Bring it on.* Autism doesn't scare me. It pisses me off sometimes. It makes me sad. It makes me frustrated and lonely and challenged but it does not end my life. It does not stunt my daughter, because she is still laughing and skipping and loving, really loving, her life.

I'm not fighting autism. I'm also not inviting it over to dinner. But it has not prevented me from seeing a magnificent life unfold and change and overcome in the span of eight short, and long, years.

Bring it.

Bring it all on, because I say *Why the hell not?*

How to Talk to an Autistic Child

by Kimberly K. Farrar

First, be still. Sit within her orbit.
Observe the way she leans into her
floppy run.

Wait.

The autistic child looks down, but sees everything:
Every glimmer in the sidewalk, every strand
of your blonde hair.

Do something physical and silent.
Make a surprised face, open your mouth
and widen your eyes.

You could nod your head or dance
a little, maybe spin slowly.
When she looks at you,
do it again.

You could try blowing
in your soda bottle to make
a deep jug sound. Be gentle.

Sit on the floor and toss a pillow.
Toss softly and say something
simple like, "Fun" or "Oh boy" or "Try again."
She may repeat what you say or stop.

If you have gotten this far, you have had
a communication. When she runs away,
let her.

A Child Blinks

by Janet Kay

AT FIRST HE SEEMED like the sun in the sky, rising on the very first morning. He had that sunshiny, storybook face—oddly vacant and fiercely penetrating at the very same time. He even cast a light like the sun for awhile, a soft inner glow the nurses referred to as jaundice. But, unlike the sun, he showed up at midnight to light the early December snows, when he ought to have been on the other side of the planet.

We named him Michael, for no one in particular, and this was duly noted on his hospital bassinet. He studied the black letters on the blue card as he lay there, his eyes open wide with surprise.

Watching him, I felt strangely pulled from my moorings to drift into new, uncharted waters. Things might be choppy up ahead, I figured, but I'd follow Michael anywhere he led me. Michael blinked and the wave crested anew. I smiled and held on for the ride.

I had been here once before, in this strange maternal otherworld, where women seemed to lose themselves forever to their children. I closed my eyes and thought of my daughter, so grown up at home—my little Jen, kneeling on her chair at the breakfast table. *Mommy, can I have a cup of honey?* I opened my eyes again and discovered she'd been replaced.

There was Michael, instead, my little orange boy, still fixated on his name card. I knew from experience how to care for him. And I knew that, whether I bathed him right or smiled enough of the time, he'd still grow up as his sister had, spinning around the kitchen on long legs, asking endless questions to amuse and annoy me.

In a day I'd go home to all that. I'd rejoin the real world again with its piles of laundry and doctor bills and dishes piling up in the sink. Only Michael would redefine the real world as I knew it, testing conventional wisdom, defying natural laws, redrawing the pathways of normal child development to suit himself.

Within a month, he would tuck his own baby blanket around his tiny body and set out to order his world. Soon he'd be counting real numbers. Then he would sort his mixed vegetables. He would teach himself to read.

I never once bragged about Michael's genius. Because, for every accomplishment I could list in his first years, there was another critical failing. All the really important things my maternal touch should have taught him—kindness, empathy, self-control—these things went unlearned. For Michael made it clear from the very start that he did not require touch like most babies did, that cuddling and crooning after his bath were as ludicrous to him as they were painful.

So I left him alone, like the sun in the sky, and I let him watch over things, and rise and set when he chose to. I studied him—worshipped him—and tried to learn his methods from afar. As a parent, my best teacher would always be my son.

In our living room the baby books sit on the shelf next to the old family Bible. Jen and Michael flip through them on lazy Saturdays, while King James rests undisturbed. Our children are too self-absorbed right now to be bothered with thou-shalt-nots.

My husband and I have found it much more effective to practice the "thou-shalt" method of parenting anyway: Be hospitable, we teach our kids. Laugh a lot. Be kind to people who need you. On the road of life, force others to love you honestly.

If only it were so easy. The road of life has been hard for our family, nearly impassable at times. It has been marked with clinical charts and disclaimers put up like roadblocks in our way. Words like Autism, Asperger's, Pervasive Developmental Disorder are always lurking around the bend as reminders of the child our Michael will never be.

Though he counted and read early, Michael didn't bother telling us. In fact, he didn't bother telling us much at all. His earliest words and phrases came two years too late and were comprised of clipped consonants, scant vowels, and very little information. The mantra "A sun my eyes" was first used on sunny days and later for all days outside. The phrase "A Bonnie" first described our cat, but was later used to talk of any animal. The surprising words, "Two three," were spoken over and over for twenty minutes straight as one-year-old Michael built a tower out of twenty-three blocks. It was the last time we would hear him speak for years.

But the truly troubling part of Michael's disability was always his nonverbal attempts to communicate: running away, screaming at close range, throwing things. Once, after hurtling a chair at a preschool classmate, Michael cried for an hour before he managed to find words for his remorse. "I didn't know a chair could break," he said.

Years later at school, he snuck an extra ravioli from the lunch line and hid it in the pocket of his pants. At recess, his teacher caught him trying to bury the evidence. Lacking an appropriate response, Michael simply growled at his teacher.

We allow ourselves to laugh behind our hands. There is, after all, a funny misdirection that courses through Michael's mind. His actions are as stupefying to us as the consequences of those actions are to him. Furthermore, the "real world" is just as ridiculous, as Michael is quick to point out. "Look," he said recently as we were riding in the car. "There's a professional building. The other buildings must feel so inferior."

It lightens his load and ours to have so refreshing an outlook. But there's still a tragic side to all this. And for Michael, the real tragedy lies in the diagnosis itself. He'd rather stumble through life without it. Often he'll be seen darting through halls at school like he's being chased by a gunman. Or sometimes he insists we take a complex driving route, so that someone who knows him won't see him. Perhaps if he moves fast enough around corners, his diagnosis won't catch up with him.

After all, what has autism ever done for him? Michael's been running from the disabling trappings of his diagnosis for his entire life. He'd rather have friends, thank you very much, than adults following him around with clipboards.

And he's had plenty of adults with clipboards trying to pave his way with their good intentions. They're eager to help, they always say, and come armed with a solid book-knowledge of autism. But their practicum with Michael leaves them cold. Because, in spite of an abundance of literature on the subject, there is no clear road map for communicating with an autistic child. So Michael's emotional language remains entrenched in concrete expressions that mean little to the rest of the world. "I'm a tiger," he said once, to describe his excitement over a gift. But the phrase could have easily meant, instead, that he was hungry or angry, or that he'd just been to the dentist, and his teeth felt clean and sharp.

Only Michael can teach the nuances of this strange language to others, and only the most patient students can learn it. In our experience, classroom teachers aren't often the best students. Michael seems combative to those who don't "get" him. When he gets that way, his teachers get angry. When his teachers get angry, Michael shuts down. Communication ceases, behavior escalates, parents are called, and blame is assigned.

My husband and I have had to shoulder most of that blame. And, like an overstuffed duffel bag, the weight of it never seems to get any lighter. I'm still reeling from the meeting I had years ago with a grade-school principal who thoughtlessly compared Michael's behavior to that of children exposed to drugs *in utero*. Or the time a teacher laughed openly at autism jokes made by her pet student in our company. Then there was the counselor who told us we were negligent for failing to put Michael on a dangerous anti-psychotic drug. And still another who chided us when we did.

We could list a hundred such teachers and administrators all too eager to lead us out the door. To date, Michael has been suspended from every school he's attended—six in all—and from every daycare center before that. The issues and administrators blur into one. So do the parents who crossed to the other side of the street when we passed.

These people are not monsters. They're good people with whom we might socialize if things were different. But they cannot accept our son's alternate reality. Frustrated, they let their uprightness slide for just a second when they're around us, long enough to dump a new load of accusations into our already-bulging duffel bag. They never even know how much it kills us.

No one knows. No one ever sees when we start to break beneath the load. Because we cry for our son in the same way we love him. We cry in secret.

There are others crying along with us: the rare school administrator who has taken years to forge a trust with Michael, the gifted teacher who has learned to play by his rules, the patient grandparents who have come to accept his emotional absence as a legitimate inborn trait. In return, these secret saints have glimpsed the strange boy living beneath the label. A few have even received his empty hug. They know how much his small affections mean.

The secret people give alms quietly, almost divinely, letting Michael lean on them like his baby book leans on the shelf—rigid, closed, his spine turned outward to guard the vulnerable story inside. You can't love a kid like that directly. You can only love him from a distance, in the dark, at night. When his face glows fair against his pillow, when the clock bends its rhythm to his beating heart.

And when, with the sun, Michael's eyes blink open, the world is redefined. He pulls himself up and stretches his gangly frame to the end of his bed. It has been a long time, these fourteen years, and yet it has passed like a day.

There is much for Michael to do this morning. There is a picture he wants to draw. There is a joke forming in the back of his mind. There is an adoring sister who will drive him to the mall if he but asks her. And, yes, there is a God, whose communication is so cryptic that some might call *Him* autistic. So I listen hard when I pray. And, because God has a sense of humor, he answers me through Michael, who's walking down the driveway, following Jen to her car. "Wouldn't it be a riot," he says, "if you honked your horn, and instead of 'beep-beep,' it said 'meow?'" Jen laughs and asks him where he came from.

I've wondered that myself at times. He is far too fresh to have sprung from this earth. He's too marvelous for my words.

The Real World of Autism: The Refrigerator Mother Club

by Chantal Sicile-Kira

IT HAPPENS TO US all. At some point or another, we become members of a club we never dreamed of joining. Membership is bestowed on us whether we want it or not. Take the Getting Old Club. No one wants to join this one, and membership is not bestowed upon you graciously as it is for prestigious country clubs. Those kinds of clubs usually send a distinguished Board Member to call on you after having received your application including references from two club members in good standing and a check for half your net worth. "Hello, Winthrop Hamilton III here. May I please speak to Joe Smith? I'd like to extend an invitation to you to join the Silver Woods Country Club. You've been nominated by two of our illustrious club members."

Membership to the clubs you don't want to join are often gradual and kind of creep up on you so that you become a member without even noticing it. When you are in the Getting Old Club, you wake up feeling stiff and your joints are creaky. You realize that supermarket checkout clerks refer to you as "sir" or "ma'am" and insist you need help out to the car with your two bags of groceries.

However, membership in this club is preferable to the alternative: membership in the Six Feet Under Club, where relatives can come and visit you at your last resting place whenever they please and stay as long as they like.

I never wanted to be a member of the Refrigerator Mother Club, but I found myself in it, nonetheless. We were living in Paris at the time, and my son who was born there was showing autistic tendencies early on. My indoctrination was quick and my membership was short. "Your son is not showing autistic tendencies," the medical professional told me, "He is just showing 'troubles de comportment' (troubles in behaving). You must take him to see a psychoanalyst."

Having taught autistic adolescents as well as counseled parents of developmentally disabled children in America before using those same skills to teach French executives business English, I was familiar with the effective methods of helping children with autism. Although I was raised bilingual and bicultural in Ohio and New York by my French parents, I wasn't familiar with the apparent cultural differences in medical treatment in general and in diagnosing and treating autism specifically. At the time, in 1990, most countries recognized autism as a developmental disability, but it was still considered a mental illness in Paris, with psychoanalysis being the only treatment on offer. I knew from my professional experience in the states that psychoanalysis was not going to do my nonverbal autistic baby any good, but my philosophy is, when in Paris do as the Parisians do. So I decided to go ahead and take Jeremy to see a psychoanalyst. Besides, the "Powers That Be" were threatening to cut off the little help I was getting for my son unless I followed the prescribed "treatment" of psychoanalysis.

The first time I went with my two-year-old son, the psychoanalyst opened the door and bid us come in. Seeing me visibly shudder as I saw shelves full of books by Bruno Bettleheim (father of the "refrigerator mother" theory of autism, which blamed cold, unloving mothers for their child's autism) she immediately stated that she did not follow or necessarily believe Bettleheim's theories, but read him. She said that, knowing I was raised in America, I was probably not in agreement with him and probably followed more the behavioral theories, but that did not fit into the French mentality. The psychoanalyst was right, the French are much too individualistic and emotional to stick to a reinforcement schedule. Think about it: a country that has its roots in existentialist philosophy and believes that your destiny is predetermined at birth, and that "Plus ça change, plus c'est la même chose"—"The more it changes the more it stays the same"—is not a country that believes that writing up behavioral goals and objectives is going to change one's preordained lot in life.

The third and last time I visited the analyst's office with my son, my husband came with us. Our little boy picked up a pair of rounded toy salt and pepper shakers and their holder, an exact replica of those you find on cafe tables. Jeremy stared at the rounded salt and pepper shakers as he rocked back and forth, seemingly impervious to all going on around him. He held them tight and twirled one of the shakers, concentrating.

"You are spinning that object. Why are you spinning the object?" the psychoanalyst asked my son.

"Because he likes to spin things, obviously," I thought, trying to count how many Bruno Bettelheim books were on the shelf. My husband (Jeremy's father) glanced at his watch, wondering how we had gotten roped into this.

"There are two of them. Two round objects. Do they remind you of your mother's breasts, Jeremy?" asked the psychoanalyst. She then turned to me and inquired, "Madame Sicile-Kira, did you breastfeed Jeremy?"

"Yes, I did," I replied, alarm bells going off in my head. At this point I felt as if I were a character in a Woody Allen movie and I knew just how the rest of the scene would play out.

"For how long?" the psychoanalyst asked me.

"About four months," I replied.

Suddenly, one of the shakers fell out of the holder in Jeremy's hands, dropped onto the wooden floor, and rolled under a piece of furniture. "Oh, you've lost one, you've lost one of your mother's breasts," cried the psychoanalyst.

I instinctively clutched my breasts to make sure they were still there. They were. Both of them. I could not look at my husband; I knew we would both burst out laughing.

"And was it a difficult separation?" the psychoanalyst asked.

"No, I don't think so—not to my recollection. Everything went smoothly," I replied.

"Oh, look!" exclaimed the psychoanalyst, observing Jeremy crawling past, chasing after the missing shaker. "He is searching, he is looking for the lost breast, his mother's breast!" she cried. "Oh, he has found it," she said, relief in her voice.

I, on the other hand was extremely thrilled, but not because my son had found my lost breast. I was happy because this was the first time my son had gone looking for an object that had disappeared out of his sight. As child development experts know (including mothers), this is an important stage that my son should have reached months ago and had not entered until now.

I never received a bill for this particular session, nor did the psychoanalyst's office ever call me back for another appointment. I can only fathom that the psychoanalyst quickly realized that I wasn't going to accept membership into the Refrigerator Mother Club, no matter how tempting it was to find something to blame for my son's autism.

Watching My Son Watch Sleeping Beauty

by Anjie Kokan

"RED MOUTH," HE SAYS to the mirror after he draws a jagged outline 'round his small and serious lips with his sister's cherry-scented marker. He's in love with a cartooned blonde who dances barefoot to "Once Upon a Dream."

"Red mouth, red mouth," he shows me as he subtly licks the animated smile on his TV. Next he puts his two index fingers together to make the sign for "feet." He must rewind back to the close-up feet scene a couple of more times before he will join the next step of this dance.

He laughs among the animated woods without borders, where jackrabbits hop in old boots, and the wild gold-eyed owl, centered in a cloak, sways with the winged beat of whistling blue birds. All the animals are happy, and the girl is happy, too, as grass tickles her leaping feet and her lovely red mouth sings of things that are seldom what they seem.

My boy's small feet are barefoot as well, with their own dancing song, and a red, red mouth that holds kisses just for me. Tell me, tell me, how can I not dance, too?

Sometimes, Never

by Susan Segal

SOMETHING IS WRONG. YOU know there is something. This is your first and only-born; still, you know. He came out round-headed and perfect, grasped your breast and heart, and burrowed his permanent way there. You want to believe that your child is like all the others—perfect in every way—that it is you who is deficient. There is nothing wrong, you try to tell yourself.

You get thrown out of grocery stores and baby gyms. You have to leave birthday parties dragging a screaming toddler behind you. You don't dare hire a babysitter for fear of 911 calls, or that she will tell you she is busy from now till the end of her days, and really, have you considered that maybe there is something ever-so-slightly *wrong* with your child?

You know there is something wrong. With The Baby. With you.

You ask the pediatrician. The conversation goes something like this:

You: I think there may be something wrong. I've been reading some books. . . .

Him: (It is a him, 60-ish, bearded, a grandfather, seasoned, advocates folk-remedies over antibiotics—you always liked that about him but now it makes him too sanguine, you think) Oh, books. Those books scare you more than help you. Look at him. He's fat, he's smiling, he's a happy kid. Go home and don't worry.

You: But…he…Does it usually take till over age four to get over the terrible twos?

Him: What did I tell you? Those books will make you crazy.

You: I . . .

Him: Yes? (He is wrestling with The Baby over the stethoscope; he looks a bit alarmed at the strength of The Baby's grip. The Baby is laughing.)

You: He has always been like this. Remember the colic?

You know he doesn't remember. He has doubled his patient load since he started accepting HMOs. He would be hard pressed to remember your name if asked. But you have forgotten nothing. Of course, it is you who stayed up night after night, pacing the floor with a screaming, sweat-grimed wild thing, who would not be consoled with singing, with patting, with mindless gibberish, and who, if you sat down for even a moment, there at 3 a.m. with your back aching and your C-section scar swelling, managed to raise the pitch to something dogs in the next town could hear, so that you had to rise again to walk, ever walk and sing and cry yourself, quietly, into his wispy hair, your tears mingling with the sheen of sweat that covered him as he shrieked.

You have not forgotten how your husband (who is no longer your husband, because, he said, he was no longer appreciated, even though you know it is because he can see himself in The Baby's affronted eyes) would finally come throttling down the stairs, squinting at the two of you as if he were nearsighted. How he'd open his mouth and close it again a few times as The Baby wailed on, finally saying, in a low, clenched voice, Do you realize that I have to get up at five o'clock in the morning? (the "o" sounding like a strangled moan). How your eyes would fill and you would begin a monologue of your helplessness, but he'd hold up his hand palm out, a traffic cop's gesture. Just get the vacuum cleaner, he'd say and stomp back up.

But the vacuum cleaner was the last resort.

Daddy has to work you'd say to The Baby's scrunched-up face, Shhh, Baby, you'd say, we're waking up daddy, shhh. As if on cue, The Baby would pause for a moment, his face slackening, perhaps considering the wisdom of silence under these circumstances, perhaps considering how best to express just what he (and secretly you, too) thought of daddy's need for sleep, and then, as

if refreshed, he'd begin anew, and so you would, in the end, opt
for the magic bullet.

Balancing The Baby over your shoulder like a sack of rice, you'd
pull out the vacuum cleaner, plug it in and turn it on and then The
Baby of the bottomless scream would go limp, as if you'd hit him over
the head with a mallet. His eyes would close, his body go slack, and
he would be blissfully quiet. You could sit at last, collapse into the
leather armchair and hold him, damp and lifeless against your chest.
Close your own eyes and breathe. Soon, though, as the vacuum cleaner roared its white noise, you'd worry about the motor burning out,
the carpet singeing, the house going up in flames. And from upstairs,
invariably, your husband would bellow, How the hell am I supposed
to sleep? Move the goddamn vacuum cleaner somewhere else.

You remember everything.

You remember calling the pediatrician's office in tears, saying,
He must be in pain, there must be something you can do, and the
doctor (who at least took your call, which you understand is a rar-
ity these days) telling you that colic had to run its course, but that
possibly you were eating something that was upsetting The Baby's
stomach. So you gave up peanuts and broccoli and cauliflower, and
when that didn't help, you added milk and cheese and fruit to the list
and before long you were down to eating only oatmeal and boiled
chicken and The Baby wailed on.

Maybe you should stop breast-feeding, your husband said. We
weren't breast-fed; we came out fine.

You're allergic to shellfish, you said. I can't eat strawberries.

Coincidence, he said.

Maybe I should stop breast-feeding, you told the pediatrician,
feeling as if you were offering him one of your vital organs.

Maybe you should, he said.

You've never forgiven him for that, not really.

So you wore cabbage leaves in your nursing bra to help with
engorgement and you bought a powdery formula that you secretly
suspected was made of pure sugar, lining up two bottles at night for
midnight and two a.m. feedings.

The Baby wailed on.

Try giving him a little coffee, the doctor says.

Excuse me?

Coffee. My mother used to give it to me when I got a little wild. It just might calm him down.

Uh huh, you say.

You are not at all sure that he's still of sound mind.

He has rescued his stethoscope from The Baby 's grasp, only because The Baby has lost interest and is now standing on the examining table, toes crunching the sheet of tissue paper covering it.

No jumping, Baby, you say, reaching for him. He smiles at you, all his chiclet Baby teeth gleaming, his perfect green eyes twinkling, the smile that has not lost its ability to set you aglow.

And he jumps.

In the parking lot you rest your head on the steering wheel. You would like to cry, but you are too exhausted. The Baby is pasting his four stickers on the backs of the car seats. He was only supposed to take one sticker from the nurse's basket, but he let it be known that the consequences of such perceived miserliness would not be pretty for anyone, and so now four Star Wars figures are gracing your car seats. You know, Mommy, he says, the ad for the movie is wrong, because Anakin Skywalker doesn't have a green light saber, he has a blue one. It's Yoda who has the green one, and then Anakin's goes red when he goes to the dark side and the other Jedi have green or blue. Did you know that Mama? Did you?

You marvel for the thousandth time how he can know so much about movies he's never seen. It's either a form of weird genius, or bad influence from the preschool. Either way, it's another thing you have failed to protect him from.

How interesting, you manage, then hold your breath. And it begins. A disquisition on the minutiae of everything from Darth Vader's breathing helmet to Luke Skywalker's muscles, a monologue punctuated by questions he's asked a million times before. Why is Darth Vader bad? Who does Yoda fight in episode three? Why doesn't Luke grow up with Leia? You have answered them a million times before, too. You don't, as your ex-husband does, tell him to knock it off, tell him to talk about something else, because you want him to feel that what interests him interests you. You don't want to let on to him that he is boring.

You decide to switch pediatricians.

He's a boy, your ex-husband says when you try to get him to share your panic.

He's only four and a half.

We should consider spanking, he says.

Remember, he's no longer your husband.

The night you asked him to leave, your husband held a plate over your head and made as if to smash it down on the softest part of your skull. As The Baby becomes not a Baby you wonder if you should have let him.

At night The Baby sleeps with all the beauty and softness of a child in a diaper commercial. You stare down at his pursed lips and perfect ears and you are flooded with love so intense that it feels like strength even though it is the very thing that renders you powerless.

Every morning that you drop him at preschool he clutches your hand in his and kisses it fervently. Then he runs off to the playground without a backward glance, waving his arms in the air. "Anakin, we're losing power!" he cries.

White slips of paper come home from the preschool. They are called Incident Reports.

"The Baby pulled another child's hair when the child wouldn't give him a truck. Action taken: The Baby was told 'no hair pulling' and separated from the other child."

"The Baby walked up to another child and bit her with no provocation. Action taken: The Baby was told 'no biting,' and given a time-out. The other child was given ice and TLC."

"Action taken: The Baby was told 'You have to share' and re-moved from the situation."

"Action taken: The Baby was sent to the office for a cool-down."

The school's director, a grandmother with a huge bosom and stick legs, mans the office. When you go there to pick The Baby up, she takes your elbow and brings you into the bathroom, where The Baby, sitting in a tiny blue time-out chair and running a toy car back and forth across a little table, can't hear you. Have you ever, she says, sotto voce, considered having him assessed?

This is how The Baby gets mad: a series of loud breaths—a sort of controlled hyperventilating, an outraged cry and then a lunge at you, head lowered. He aims for the stomach; his hands rake your arms. When you hold him off, his mouth goes for your wrists, your legs, whatever bare skin is available. Sometimes he is successful. You have tri-colored bruises on both thighs from where his teeth have successfully sunk in. Twice he's broken the skin. The long thin scratches on your neck look like you've taken a red marker to it. Sometimes he just takes a handful of your cheek and digs in his nails, twisting. These moves still shock and surprise you, so often you are undefended. Can a child so small cause so much pain?

Over the phone, your ex-husband says, He never acts that way with me. What is wrong with you?

You press the phone into your ear and accidentally brush the scratch The Baby left on the side of your cheek.

Ouch, you say.

This is how your ex-husband would get mad: He'd slam things. Cabinets, doors. He cursed. He bought packs of cigarettes and smoked them furiously on the back patio. He would disappear for hours at a time, and come home, silent, pouting, and go to bed.

You used to try to talk to him when he'd calmed down. He would get mad all over again. Inevitably at that moment The Baby would fall out of bed, or tip his rocking chair over, or deliberately knock his head against the wall just to see what it felt like. Now, apparently, your ex is a model father and has created a part-time angelic child.

You read a parenting book that says The Baby is going through a phase and that if you visualize yourself as a better parent you can actualize it. You close your eyes and see yourself floating down a pristine river, the air crisp and cool, the scent of evergreens and roses emanating from the shore, a diaphanous gown swirling around you, and for a moment you are uplifted until you realize that you are imagining yourself as Ophelia.

This is how you get mad: First, you fall silent. Sometimes you don't say three words in three days. The Baby crawls into your lap then, and strokes your hair. You can't help it. You flinch.

One of your best friends works at the preschool. She's the mother you wanted to be. She never says no to her two angels. You do it like this, she says: Instead of saying No standing on the furniture you say Feet on the floor please. Instead of saying No hitting you say It hurts when you hit. Your friend's biggest family issue is the fact that she has no interest in sex and as a result her husband engages in various passive-aggressive behaviors like starving the dog and using the last roll of toilet paper.
I am not the mother I wanted to be, you tell her.
She says something that at first strikes you as wise and then floods you with so much guilt that you are struck dumb with failure.
She says: He is not the child you wanted him to be.

When your ex-husband comes to pick up The Baby you tell him that the director of the preschool recommended that The Baby get tested. He snorts. Tested for what? he says. The kid is four.
You nod. You have to agree. There was a time when you, too, were a rational person. When you read and approved of articles about overly medicated children and reviews of books about how modern society pathologizes boys. Now you are one of the converted. Your boy is your religion now.
You need to relax, your ex-husband says. Get in the car, already, he says crisply to The Baby and The Baby does, just like that.
You blink. I am relaxing, you say.

You call your doctor's office. What is it regarding, the officious nurse asks.

I need to relax, you say.

Uh huh, the nurse says.

Tentatively, you say, I'm interested in medication.

What kind? she says.

Something slams into your buttocks and you wheel around. It's The Baby's head.

I'm hungry, he growls. I'm Chewbacca, and I want some MEAT!

I'll have to call you back, you say to the nurse.

The next day you go down to the school district office and fill out a pile of forms. We will notify you within 30 days when we will assess him, says the lady at the front desk.

On one form it asks questions like these: Does your child act as if he has a motor running all the time? Always, sometimes, never? Does your child easily get stuck on one topic? Does your child have violent outbursts? Always, sometimes, never?

Your hand shakes as you check off more boxes than can be normal. You try to swallow the clump in your throat. You imagine that with every box you check you are betraying your child and yourself. You are admitting to the world that your child is unmanageable. You are admitting that you have failed: as a mother. As a wife.

From the district office you drive to The Baby's preschool. He's on the playground, his teacher says, He had a pretty good day today. Only one tantrum, and we caught him twice before he bit.

When The Baby sees you, he runs to you and leaps into your arms. Your chest constricts with pleasure. You breathe in his smell, that peculiar blend of baby shampoo, dirt, and something sweet, like playdough, or children's glue. He nuzzles your neck and tells you he drew a picture of his family today. Daddy was in it too, he says.

You laugh and wonder if you just made a huge mistake filling out those forms. Watching him wiggle with delight at the sight of you, it is hard to imagine that he would ever sink his teeth into you.

The Baby takes your hand and practically drags you to the car. All the way home he chatters about Luke and Leia, Obi Wan, and what he had for snack that day. You nod and smile, and comment when he lets you, and as you drive you begin to feel as if you are floating again, but this time, upwards—as if you've driven the car up above the streets, as if you and The Baby are sailing over the tops of the buildings. From up here the only sound is The Baby's chattering voice—all the ones that rant in your head are silent, and you and he are on your way to somewhere new and unknown. You find yourself wondering vaguely if you will be able to come down eventually—or if you will want to. You ask yourself the following question: Will today be the day you can start being the mother you wanted to be?

Always, sometimes, never.

PART II

String Theory

String Theory

by Emily Willingham

MY SON'S NAME IS Thomas Henry. He was born on May 4, 2001, and by accident, we named him after Thomas Henry (T.H.) Huxley, who also was born on May 4, but in 1825. Huxley's distinction was earning the epithet "Darwin's bulldog" after distinguishing himself in a great debate about evolution. We came up with our own TH's name long before his birth, not knowing there was another, more-famous TH who shared not only the name, but the birthday.

To add to the auspices surrounding our son's birth, we selected as his godfather a man whose career is one seemingly smooth path of success: lettering in track, Ivy League B.A., top of his class at a top law school, partner in his firm at a tender age. We didn't know it at the time, but his birthday also happens to be…May 4. And he was just diagnosed at age 40 as having Asperger's.

Our own TH received his diagnosis at age 4.

TH would see all these fours in his life and think that they were good numbers. He finds some numbers quite attractive, and although he likes the number 4, his favorite number is 8. The draw of the number 8 lies in its relationship to the infinite. It just goes on and on, looping around and around, crossing and recrossing, no beginning, no end.

I was delighted to find that we had accidentally named our son after Darwin's bulldog, delighted that our TH shared a birthday with the more famous TH. For me, this connection, however random, however coincidental, is as significant as an eagle flying aloft was for the ancient Greeks. I see in this connection a portent, one of those inexplicable, random-seeming links between things unrelated except for their mutual relevance to Me or to Us.

In spite of this apparently irrational feeling, I am a scientist, a worshipper at the altar of the scientific method, one who believes in the three Es: experience, empiricism, and evidence. I'm geek enough about science even to have a favorite equation, one that for me ties together all that is important about life, the universe, and everything. That equation is Newton's Law of Universal Gravitation.

I know that for many people, using terms like "equation" or "universal gravitation" or even "Newton" can make the eyes glaze over, the synapses fritz, the interest level bottom out to zero. But zero is exactly where this equation can never go.

The equation looks like this: $F_{gravity} = G \, m_1 \times m_2/d^2$

In the denominator of the equation sits distance. We all probably remember that a denominator can't be zero. But even more relevant to this equation is that this measure of distance is between two objects. Obviously, if the distance between two objects becomes zero, they are no longer two, they are one.

The two objects under consideration provide the numerator of the equation—the "top part." Here is where we put the mass of the two objects—for example, my mass (which will remain a state secret) and the mass of the moon (which is about 7.36×10^{22} kilograms). The moon and I are mutually attracted to each other, which probably explains a lot, and that mutual attraction between us is gravitational force. Any two things with mass have this attraction and are at some nonzero distance from one another. Since every thing has mass and any two things must have distance between them to *be* two, gravitational force can't possibly be zero.

You'll notice that I've only mentioned the masses of two objects (m_1 and m_2) and the distance (which is sitting there on the bottom, squared). I haven't mentioned that big ol' G sitting there. Obviously, that stands for GRAVITY. It's a proportional constant, meaning it is set as a standard and remains constant across the universe, kind of like God in a way—omnipresent (all over the universe) and omnipotent (a power that exists over everything with mass). Take any two things with mass, throw in the constant, and divide by the distance (squared), and you've divined the magnitude of the force between those things. That force will never be zero. G, like God, will always be there. And there will be an attraction, no matter how minute.

This force of attraction, like so many other forces of attraction, grows with proximity. When it comes to gravitational affinity, distance does not make the bond grow stronger.

There are four people in the world with whom I share the strongest human affinity, the bonds of love. No equation could define the strength of this attachment, the power of that force that binds me to them. Not even G can encompass all the elements that tie us together. Some can be quantified, the way we quantify $F_{gravity}$. We could count the nucleotides in our DNA, measure our relatedness, even quantify the evolutionary drives that motivate us. But when love is infinite, no equation is necessary. A simple number 8, turned sideways, suffices.

Before we knew anything about Asperger's or autism, we knew TH. He was our "naturalist savant," the child who could name the flora around us with better memory than his botany-challenged mother. His earliest obsession was acorns, which drew him with their insignificant masses the way negative draws positive on a pair of magnets. He could home in on these tiny oak progeny with inerrant precision, collecting them by the hundreds, forming swirling patterns on the floor with them, creating his earliest version of infinity with these representatives of infinite life: the seed. TH would scream out "acorns!" in a crowded park the way most children would scream out "ice cream!" when seeing the object of their desire.

This unifocal obsession planted some of the first seeds of suspicion in our minds about TH and Asperger's. A simple Google search on obsession, squealing, hand flapping, meltdown, and voila! The hits start coming…autism, Asperger's, spectrum. A mother's mind might reel, except that I, the mother, already knew that TH was an unusual, an exceptional child. In fact, it came as no surprise to me that the child of my heart fell onto this spectrum we all talk about in the world of autism. I didn't have a moment where I felt that I had "lost my child." There were no cherished dreams I'd prematurely transmogrified into realities, no air castles to deflate, no pies to drop from the sky. I knew the minute I read the criteria in the *Diagnostic and Statistical Manual of Mental Disorders* (DSM IV) that someone seemed to have been thinking of TH when they wrote them. It didn't change one single thing about my son to know that. He was still TH, still the botanist savant with a thing for acorns and the occasional burning desire to sleep with a boiled egg. Still the child who loves the number 8.

So when the developmental pediatrician whom we'd paid $600 (TH does not like 6 so much) for the privilege gave her final pronouncement, I didn't flinch. I didn't cry. I simply picked up the phone and began to call all of the various therapists she had recommended so we could get TH rolling on the smoothest path we could forge for him. There's a law of motion related to that metaphor, more fruit of the mind of Isaac Newton, describing the way an object in motion will stay in motion unless an outside force interferes. Our goal was to protect TH from the interacting forces of society, the "neurotypical" expectations that could broadside him and shift him off of the happy trail he'd always trod.

Through hours of OT and speech therapy, through a few half-hearted attempts with a psychotherapist, I stayed with this child. Rochester in *Jane Eyre* speaks of having "a string somewhere under my left ribs, tightly and inextricably knotted to a similar string in the corresponding quarter of your little frame." Of course, he speaks to the woman he loves. But I have four of those strings, each one leading from that beating heart under my left ribs to my husband and the little frames of each of my three sons. During those days with TH, this string pulled tight, drawing my heart taut with anxiety and worry. I worried it would break, that somehow, I would lose this happy, funny, hand-flapping connoisseur of acorns. I worried that either the world would intrude and knock him from his blissfully unaware path or that autism would intrude and toss up obstacles we could not yet foresee. That he would stumble, suffer an incurable pain of the psyche or the soul. That he would change.

In hindsight, I know that no matter what your child is like, things can and likely will change. Happy, neurotypical children can grow into depressed adults. Obstacles and traps lie in wait out there that have nothing to do with autism. No one can see around the turns in the trail. No one has the power to burn a clear view through the fog of the future. TH could be the most neurotypical child in the world, and I'd still feel that string pull taut on many an occasion.

Our road to diagnosis was quick, probably too fast and free of obstacles for my husband, I think. This road followed a chain of events that in retrospect seemed almost guided, mapped out for us. TH selected as his closest friend in preschool the son of a speech-language pathologist. She provided a ten-minute screening at the school one day and communicated her concerns about TH's results in a two-page letter. Our personal connection made things smoother in many ways: we trusted her at the outset and she gave us good recommendations for people to do further evaluations. To this day, we stay in touch with her, this person who forged the first key to unlocking the mysteries of what was going on with our son. We no longer live near their family, feeling the connective force of proximity, but we created a different sort of connection, one that Newton never mapped out in an equation.

TH kept up some of his mysterious behaviors into kindergarten, including his tendency to isolate himself in unstructured group situations, exploring the periphery of any area alone, examining everything in minute detail. Yet somehow, he managed to form another friendship, attracting yet another perfect companion whose family would turn out to be another blessing for us. We reflect on this path we've followed with TH, these encounters with exactly the right people at exactly the right time in our lives. These encounters were never obstacles; they were always signposts, and we can't help but feel a guiding hand behind it, something besides us that smoothes this path, easing us over the dips and bumps. There is no equation that I know that explains it, and I'm that worshipper of science, the woman who has a favorite physics equation. Perhaps there's a universal G that works on us in ways that have nothing to do with the laws of physics.

The universal G was at work again, pulling TH and this new kindergarten friend together, two little blond, beautiful boys, hard to tell apart in appearance, but clearly different in behavior. His friend has a younger brother with special needs that are very similar in many ways to TH's. This family, with such understanding and sympathy, was the first ever to invite TH for a play date, to have him for a sleepover, to take him in and behave just as if he were one of their own. I can still feel the tears come when I think of how incredible it was that *our TH* was having a *sleepover*, already, at age five. Casually, just like "regular" people. Exceeds expectations, indeed.

TH often effaces the law of universal gravitation by reducing the distance between him and his friend to zero, constantly grabbing impulsively in big hugs, violating too often the "body bubble" that defines everyone's personal space. But the friend tolerates it. He's used to it because his little brother does it all the time, too. The other kids at school naturally become annoyed with TH when he grabs them like this. But this friend seems to have infinite patience with our little boy, the child who simply can't resist the force of attraction and must express himself with that physical contact.

This child of my heart does the same to me. I begin every day with a suddenness that is more alarming than an alarm clock. Each morning, TH breaks through my deep sleep with a thud, entering my room, pausing at the doorway, and then, as though overwhelmed by some forceful impulse, he rushes to my bed and leaps on me, placing his favorite fuzzy blanket on my head. This is our ritual in the morning. I overcome this unnerving awakening almost instantly and welcome him, listening to him get out his morning purring and vocalizations, letting him get some sensory input from me as we snuggle. Our connection is so strong that even with this zero distance between us, as I lie there at dawn with my firstborn baby now grown so big in my arms, that little tether under my left ribs still feels stretched tight, straining with the power of the love I feel for this child.

If I feel such a tug on that cord even without distance between us, I don't want to imagine what it will feel like when the distance becomes real, maybe due to a first field trip out of town, or a high-school trip, or college. Or marriage. Or a job in another part of the world. I know that string will pull tighter than I've yet experienced. But just as Newton predicts, no matter how great the distance grows between us, there is a force that will still hold us together. And it's not just the universal G.

When I think of that kind of future, I like to imagine that the flexibility of that string is itself infinite. Distance has limitations. It is not infinite, certainly not here on planet Earth. TH may go far from me, geographically or mentally or just because his days become too busy. If he proves to be as successful as his godfather, not in spite of but because of his diagnosis, I will rejoice, even as that string draws taut. If he becomes another Darwin's bulldog, or even another Darwin, I will rejoice, even if it means he's away from me. There will be times, I know, that the cord may pull and tug and hurt like hell. And there will be, God willing, times that it will relax and loosen and hearts will be merry.

But one thing I know about that string: As long as I live, it will never break. No matter what distance comes between us, that force will be there, tying us together. It is my love for him, ready to take a beating or be requited, to be stretched and strained and soothed and repaired, but never to be broken or destroyed. My love for my son, like the number 8, has no beginning and no end. It just is.

Evolution of a Fairy

by Carolyn Walker

THERE GOES MY SON, his wings, the color of green beans, drooping as he slogs across the living room and kicks his sodden shoes into a pile. Behind him the train to his fairy costume, falling over the layers of sheen and silk and taffeta that he spent months sewing together by hand, sheds a streak of mud onto the carpeting. He is my Sugar Plum in from a downpour.

"A woman asked me to join her traveling fairy troupe today," he offers. Christian has been spending his summer weekends as a character at the local Renaissance Festival, where he fits in with the sword swallowers, the belly dancers, the fire eaters, the wood nymphs, the walking tree, the gypsies, the ogres and wenches, the knights and kings, and, yes, the queens, better than he has fit in anywhere in his life. As he speaks, rivulets of mascara crisscross a frosted golden face that is highlighted by ivy leaves drawn upwards from the corners of his eyes. His right eyebrow, plucked to half its original length in a fit of enthusiasm, has finally grown back in. A year ago, when he was trying to divide his uni-brow and the plucking was still fresh, it looked like the broken signal arm at a railroad crossing. When he raised his eyebrows, it went up and down in that stumpish sort of way that you imagine a broken signal arm would go. Today, though, it's back to normal, arching up into an inverted V as he presses his gaze onto me. "It's perfectly legitimate," he says. He knows me too well. "If you don't believe me, just go to www.ibelieveinfairies.com."

The fact is I don't have all that much trouble believing. I have felt the lure of fairies, and all the implications of that word, for most of Christian's life. By the time he was a toddler, it was easy to observe his tendencies—to hear his slight lisp, see the lilt in his walk and the way he floated his hands. What was much better hidden was his Asperger syndrome: That quirky little part of him that cannot...well, that cannot discern the quirky little part of him. Even as he enters adulthood, he asks me as he has so many times in the past, "What is it, Mom? What do people see in me? I don't get it."

The I-don't-get-its have presented some particularly devilish conundrums for my son. When he was a child, he didn't get why other boys wanted to play street hockey or football when he wanted to draw big red lips on the driveway, over and over. And when he was a teenager he didn't get why it was just a little weird for him to want to trick-or-treat as an Egyptian goddess. Later, when he was twenty, in the incident that most unnerved me, he didn't get why it wasn't okay for him to chase after the man who mugged him...his one-hundred-and-five pounds of skin and bones motivating themselves across a parking lot and up a street, in the bitter cold, in his shirtsleeves, on New Year's Eve, at three in the morning.

"I've had it, Mom," he told me the day after the mugging, right after he burst through the front door, broken necklace in hand, jolting me out of my reading material with, "Well, your worst fears have come true." He sliced his hand through the air to emphasize his point. "I've *had* it. I decided that I wasn't leaving until I got my money and my necklace back. I'm done being a victim."

In Christian's reality, he has been on the receiving end of more taunting and harassment than any human being should have to bear, his androgynous Aspie persona having for years presented itself as something impossibly confounding to members of the public. On New Year's Eve he had reached his threshold. The fact that his perpetrator might have had a gun or a knife or a gang of thugs waiting in the shadows did not concern him. In fact, he seemed renewed, empowered by his own actions as he reported them to me. I watched while he sat more erect, more confident. I watched his eyes transform into beads under his scowl.

According to Christian, he had meant to do a good deed when he pulled money from his wallet to give to a man asking for a handout, inadvertently wielding a $20 bill, much more than he could afford to give. In the scramble that followed, the bill had torn in half, the man had snatched his wallet, and Christian had given pursuit. When he caught up with the man, a fight ensued. My son had been held in a headlock and choked. He had elbowed his way free and snatched his wallet back. The thief had ripped a necklace from around his neck and run again. Christian had chased him a second time. The thief had threatened to shoot him if he didn't back off, but Christian didn't believe there was a gun.

He'd not felt the weight of one bumping him during the scuffle, so there must not be one, he'd reasoned.

"I'm not leaving without my money," he told the thief.

By this time, the thief had lost whatever portion of the money he had salvaged. They went their separate ways, finally, walking away from one another like two people who had been on a disastrous date.

Arrogant and determined as Christian apparently was, I had to believe that he had encountered a merciful thief, or maybe one who didn't want to add a murder to his rap sheet. In the days that followed, when I wasn't physically vibrating from the emotional fallout of his story, I wondered at what must have been the thief's surprise when a scrawny, gay, slightly autistic boy turned on him.

In my opinion, this event was only obliquely related to my son's sexual orientation. It happened outside a gay club. More importantly, I believe it happened because Christian filtered the man's need, and his own need for acceptance, through his autism. He reached to give the man a dollar, oblivious to the fact that the parade of other patrons never stopped its flow into the bar, or even acknowledged the man standing there.

Christian was born in 1987. I began to suspect he was gay on Labor Day in 1990, when, during the Jerry Lewis MDA Telethon, he raced to the hall closet to grab a bath towel, swirled it around his waist and mounted the couch, where he can-canned in sync with a bevy of Jerry's guests. He kicked his bare legs out in front of him and sashayed the towel up so that his white thighs flashed, as if he'd been sashaying since before he left the womb. I had one of those mind/body/spirit experiences Oprah likes to speak about. I felt the surge of epiphany go through me: *Christian is gay!*

I can still feel what that surge felt like. The way a burn went from my feet to head. The way my heart galloped.

As it happened, the telethon aired at about the same time Christian and I started debating whether or not he could have a dress. He began wanting one the evening his seventeen-year-old sister got gussied up for her high school homecoming. She promenaded out of her bedroom in a black sequined gown, pumps, hoop earrings, and deep red lipstick, and Christian was smitten. I didn't know it then, but I realize now, this tendency to obsess over things was linked to his Asperger's.

The next morning he began begging for a dress, any kind of dress—housedress, wedding dress, moo-moo, second-hand, even a simple A-line skirt; it didn't matter. When he watched my mother's vacation video of Greek dancers in togas his hopes were bolstered. "Those guys have dresses," he informed me solemnly. Soon I noticed he had begun sticking his superhero stickers onto his earlobes, like earrings. When he asked his sister to paint his fingernails, I compromised by letting her do the pinkies.

I remember rationalizing to myself, while telling him *no* about a dress, that it wasn't all that unusual for a small child to want to gender-bend. What does a small child know about sexuality or orientation? I thought. In my youth, I had been a terrible tomboy. I eschewed dolls and ruffles in favor of baseball, tree climbing, marble games, and fishing, in particular. My favorite clothing item was my pair of cowboy boots. My favorite toy, my wood burning set. If I could indulge in those traditionally masculine pursuits, I reasoned, why should it be a big deal for my son to show his feminine side?

Relax, I told myself. He's just a kid with a big imagination. He'll outgrow it.

Still, I remained edgy as his boyhood went by, telling myself I was a victim of stereotypes and resenting my intuition whenever it reared its head. My skin fairly rippled one day when I saw him, at age four, in the neighbor girl's driveway, wearing a pair of her mother's high-heeled shoes and slinging a patent leather purse over his arm. And I gasped out loud when our public school system mailed a calendar to every household in the district (20,000+) with a cover photo of Christian in a pink tulle skirt and vest from the preschool costume box, grinning at the camera.

In an effort to assuage my anxiety and to masculinize him, I bought him a baseball glove and a bat. I gave him Batman pajamas, complete with black cape and mask, hoping that the cape would compensate for the coveted dress. I put him in karate. I got him toy weapons, for heaven's sake: *swords* and *guns*.

All the while I had this sense that there was something different about Christian—something I couldn't quite put my finger on and the pediatrician couldn't seem to find. I was totally unaware of Asperger's existence in the world until he was diagnosed at a university hospital in 1999, when my son, a previously popular and good student, began failing his classes, crying incessantly, and exhibiting obsessive/compulsive symptoms. These behaviors showed themselves after we moved into a new house, which meant moving him to a new school, which coincided with the advent of puberty, which coincided with other boys' need to prove their mettle at someone else's expense.

Since he had been a mostly happy and agreeable little boy, I had no way of knowing that change would be profoundly difficult for Christian. Change, I've since learned, is an inherently hard process for a person on the autism spectrum. No matter what I said or did, the older he became the more resolutely he entrenched himself—and his power—in fantasy. He went through a prolonged witch phase during which he dressed in costume, drew witches prodigiously, and perfected his cackle before acquiescing to me and having a brief go as a more socially acceptable—but less satisfying—wizard, before finally giving life to the green fairy.

When it is impossible for a child to change, a mother must, I discovered. It is the only way to keep the heart whole.

I can trace the glimmerings of my acceptance of Christian's twin truths to 1997, when Death trumped me by weighing in on the side of dress-up at Christian's first funeral, that of my ninety-year-old uncle on my mother's side.

Peculiar himself, my Uncle Wally would probably be diagnosed, by modern standards, as having one or more learning disabilities, or perhaps very mild mental retardation. His eyes had an offset quality, he had slurred speech—made worse when he didn't wear his dentures—and he was limited in his academic abilities and his common sense, although he successfully held down an orderly's job at the state mental hospital near his home for thirty years.

Despite his challenges, Uncle Wally had a sentimental and generous heart. He delighted in sending Hallmark cards, handing out old silver dollars, shadow boxing, and telling tall tales—such as the one about the time he was "scouted by the big ones" after riding in the Kentucky Derby. He would slur that story to you, swaying in his seat as if he were atop a thoroughbred, then wipe tears of laughter from his perpetually watering eyes.

These were delightful traits in the eyes of my sensitive and magical little boy, who beat a path to the front door whenever Uncle Wally came to call.

Because Christian is inclined to both literal and fanciful interpretations, I knew that even at age ten he would need a young child's introduction to death. I wanted him to keep a rein on any dread he might feel and to trust that his memories and love for Uncle Wally would stay with him; to understand that death is a natural part of life, that it is something to be respected but not necessarily feared; and to remember that there is comfort in the arms of family, even when its members are grieving. As we disembarked our car in the funeral home parking lot, I chose my words to him carefully, reassuring him that Uncle Wally was at peace and that everything would be okay; then I held him by the shoulder and led him through the oak and beveled-glass doors.

Beyond them, in the foyer, was a funereal hullabaloo. My mother, who earlier in the week had been beset by a head cold, stood greeting the bereaved while wearing a blue surgeon's mask, the white strings tied up around her ears. Her hazy aquamarine eyes peered out over it, and every now and then she sniffed in, creating a pocket that was about the size of a quarter. I could hear the room's air rushing through the mask's mesh, then in and out of my mother, a sort of Mrs. Darth Vader in mourning.

Beyond her at a bit of a distance, a middle-aged spiritual advisor who wore advanced-stage Shirley Temple curls, a billowing, black, calf-length skirt, and unlaced Brogans, toured the viewing room offering words of comfort to Wally's relatives and friends. I could not quite make out her words, but her gestures—an arm around a waist, a tip of the head—seemed kind and reassuring.

Uncle Wally, dead from generalized organ failure, lay in his casket at the far end surrounded by stuffed chairs, high-shine mahogany tables, and walls adorned in pink and gold paisley wallpaper. He looked like he was made from pie dough—his skin reflecting a sort of semi-gloss white sheen—and he was wearing his navy blue Odd Fellows go-to-meeting uniform, the one with the big brass buttons. On the casket, just above his legs, where a spray of roses might have been, were his tried-and-true cowboy boots, worn crusty with age and shaped like his feet, the toes walked into hooks. My uncle loved anything that had to do with horses or the Old West and my mother apparently believed she was sending him off in a style that he would have appreciated.

Above all this, as if a host of angels had taken up yodeling, cowboy Muzak could be heard coming from the ceiling speakers. The Muzak entered the room and settled on the gathering like a spell.

With me at his side muttering about how Uncle Wally would appear asleep, Christian approached the casket tentatively, stood up on his tiptoes, and peered in without saying a word. I wondered if he was trying to reason out the fact that someone he loved had been put in a box. After a long pause, he turned his eyes to the room and my mother's theatrical spin on mourning before letting them fall on me: my eyes scanning from Wally to cowboy boots to Brogans to mask and back to Christian…to inevitability.

Ten years later, in search of mealtime conversation, I ask Christian what he recalls about Uncle Wally's funeral. I'm looking for him to confirm the overall zaniness I remember. I'm hoping he'll resurrect some tidbit I've forgotten, hoping he'll say the experience ignited his appreciation for human quirks, including his own.

It is a few months after his stint as the Renaissance fairy and we are eating sushi, his favorite, in a Japanese restaurant after his counseling appointment. He has been seeing a counselor since the taunting began in middle school, the hope being that he might learn to control the obsessive/compulsive symptoms he developed, and gain insight into the ways his feelings and thinking inform his life.

The compulsions had, and have, the effect of snap-jerking his self-acceptance and growth. He taps things. He grunts. He spins in place. He flaps his blanket over and over—all in a misguided attempt at controlling his fate. Some of the compulsions are exhausting, and some contribute to him being unnecessarily thin. He won't, for example, eat anything that is green (except broccoli and seaweed). And he believes his left hand to be cursed and therefore dangles it at his side during meals. I bring him to this restaurant weekly, hoping to tempt an appetite that is bigger than his fears.

The restaurant is decorated in classic Japanese colors and paintings, and a small pack of waiters, suggestive of ninjas in their all-black uniforms, serves the diners. One of them, who has an Elvis pompadour highlighted ketchup red and mustard yellow, has just walked by our booth. The streaks accent his forehead and light up his eyes. I point the hair out to Christian, who keeps his own hair cropped short, and covertly contemplate his features as he pivots to look—the dark brown eyes, like his father's, the beautiful smile, reminiscent of mine—and decide he is the most handsome man in the room. I watch while he uses the long, graceful fingers on his right hand to pinch his chopsticks around a piece of California roll and lift it, a big knot of crab and rice, to his mouth.

There across the table, his Asperger's and homosexuality palpable, intrinsic, mysterious as the wind, he plunks the sushi into his mouth, easy as dropping a penny into a well, and closes around it. He takes my question in whole, too. Meeting my gaze, he says he remembers that there were cowboy boots on Uncle Wally's casket. He doesn't recall the cowboy Muzak, and he doesn't remember that my mother wore a mask until I mention it.

"A mask?" he says. He looks at me harder.

"A blue surgeon's mask, remember?" I say.

He thinks for a moment, nods, says, "Oh, yes" and then, a wry afterthought: "That's Grandma!" His eyes perk and his voice carries the weight of implication, though he stops short of the comment he usually makes when we discuss her antics: *That woman is a nut job.*

Christian puts down his chopsticks, and I watch as he puffs up a bit, his lips a smug line, his chest inflated. He doesn't get the way he echoes his own tormentors. Soon he is given over to what he thinks is a change in topic. "You should see me in my fairy costume at the Renaissance Festival," he chirps. His face fairly shines with adoration for the fantasy version of himself. "It's like I'm two different people from two different worlds."

Live via Satellite: A Parenting Journey

by Mary McLaughlin

I SAW THE UNIVERSE for the first time the day my son was born. I sat in my hospital bed and stared at Bud, a tiny stranger, pink and blotchy from the work of being born, and for a few minutes he was all I could see. Then, slowly, a background began to emerge, and I saw around him a limitless universe of complexity and possibility—a universe of love and fear, of relationship and loneliness, of power and responsibility. I felt a sudden, reassuring sense of connection to this universe and a jarring flash of clarity about my small place within it. I then understood that it was my job to help Bud make his own way through it and find his own place in it.

I immediately tried to launch Bud off on the same trajectory as other children, but despite my efforts to keep him in a well-traveled orbit, he continually wandered off course, into uncharted territory. When he was an infant, I tried to take him on outings, but we seemed to spend most of our time wrestling through diaper changes in the back of our minivan, because Bud shrieked and trembled when we entered public restrooms. When Bud was a toddler, I tried pointing out rainbows, birds, and clouds to him, but he looked at my fingers instead of at the sky. When Bud was two, I tried to teach him to carry on a conversation, but though he could recite entire *Sesame Street* sketches, he wouldn't answer a yes-or-no question. When he was three, I had to hold him back from starting preschool, because even though he could surf the Internet with ease, he couldn't read his body's cues that told him when he needed to use the bathroom. It seemed the more I tried to keep Bud on course, the farther away he traveled.

I tried to enlist others to help me alter Bud's trajectory—first Bud's father and my parents; then a music teacher; then Bud's doctor; then an early intervention specialist, a speech-language pathologist, and an occupational therapist; then a developmental pediatrician— and each offered a different perspective on Bud's path until, finally, the reason for his divergence became clear: Bud had autism. He wasn't having trouble following the same orbit as his peers; he was trying to follow a different orbit altogether. I became determined to help him find one better suited to him, and together we discovered two differ- ent paths we could take, each with its own unique atmosphere: one had more gravity than we were used to, and one had less.

If we took the high-gravity orbit, we would stay grounded, but feel weighed down. Each movement would be difficult, and would take careful consideration. We'd be burdened by every decision and we'd labor through every forward step. If it didn't go well, we would become immobilized. If we took the low-gravity orbit, we would float above the ground, catching glimpses of where we wanted to land, but we would struggle to find our footing. We'd be able to go with the flow and catch new ideas in the wind, but if it didn't go well, we would lose our focus and float away.

I decided to follow Bud's lead as, without hesitation, he chose a low-gravity approach to life. He acclimated quickly, and though he bobbed and weaved, he moved clearly and determinedly forward. I took advantage of the atmosphere as well, and shot myself a little further into the sky to assume a new role in Bud's life as he traveled his chosen path. I became his satellite.

I found an orbit around Bud—close enough to have influence, far enough away to keep us from a collision course—as he followed his own trajectory, different from those of the bodies around him, moving at his own pace in his own direction. I tried to think about short-term advances, to build a force field against questions about

Bud's future that barraged us like asteroids, threatening to throw us off course: Will Bud ever have a conversation? Will he make friends? Will he finish high school? Go to college? Have a job? Fall in love? Will Bud be happy? Instead, I tried to focus on the orbit that Bud was following, and let his path through space emerge in its own time and in its own way.

In the years since Bud's diagnosis, some of my early questions have been answered. We have conversations, though they're usually peppered with quotations from his most treasured books and videos. He has friends, though having friends is not a high priority for him. The other questions have traveled into a more remote corner of the universe, and they're not as threatening as they once were.

My role as satellite, however, has expanded. It's a role I love, and it provides opportunities for work that are much more versatile and interesting than I could have imagined. Sometimes as I orbit Bud, I'm a surveillance satellite, taking pictures from space and beaming them back to the analysts on Earth. I capture and record snapshots in time, ready to transmit the data to the doctors, psychologists, educators, or therapists who need it: When did he first sit, stand, crawl, walk, speak? How does he play, relate, object, respond? What does he enjoy, dislike, seek out, avoid? I provide reams of data as we work to determine how the pieces fit together and try to make meaning of the patterns they suggest.

At other times, I'm a communications satellite, waiting for Bud to transmit messages through space to me so that I can bounce them to the people who need to receive them. I was called into action recently at Dunkin' Donuts, when Bud marched to the counter, looked the clerk square in the face, and announced in a booming script from an Oswald cartoon, "I would like a salmon sorbet, please!"

The clerk smiled nervously and shifted her questioning gaze to me.

I smiled back and clarified, "He'd like a jelly munchkin and a chocolate munchkin, please."

Message transmitted, and received.

Sometimes the job is not as much fun. One summer, Bud developed acute anxiety about thunderstorms and started to panic when dark clouds gathered. I assumed the role of weather satellite, scanning the skies for signs of inclement weather, calculating the timing, the duration, and the severity of any potential precipitation, and planning our days accordingly.

At other times, Bud's anxieties require me to become a defense satellite, watching vigilantly for potential threats on his horizon—a barking dog, a shrieking baby, a peer who demands too much, an adult who invades his personal space—and deflecting them before they are able to make contact or do damage.

In easier times, I am an entertainment satellite, beaming in the diversions that I know will bring Bud delight—a summer trip to the ocean to plunge into the icy waves; an afternoon in winter spent making snow angels. I've learned to transmit the characters and dialogues he loves most, to help his scripted echolalia transform from isolating monologue to connected conversation, as I become Bert to his Ernie, Minnie to his Mickey, or The Man with the Yellow Hat to his Curious George.

Most of the time, though, I'm a more natural satellite: a moon. My phases coordinate with Bud's as I help him regulate the tidal ebbs and flows of his engagement with the world. Sometimes, I loom large on his horizon, a visible, tangible presence, illuminating the things that surround him: "Look, Bud. See this. Do this. Care about this." Other times, I fade into the background, a faraway sliver whose influence is barely perceptible as Bud steps forward, makes his own decisions, and prepares to launch.

Together, Bud and I cycle through the phases of our lives, negotiating and renegotiating our relationship, connected and buoyed by an invisible force that keeps us in sync. Bud makes his way through the universe differently but successfully, as I orbit somewhere nearby, making the subtle and strategic modifications in my trajectory that his autism dictates. We are two bodies in gentle progression, each of us spinning on our own axis, circling each other in a complicated choreography, slowly and persistently moving forward together.

It's interesting. This low-gravity parenting journey has me floating in space, sometimes feeling light years away from the known or the familiar. And yet, as I move into the vast expanse before me, I only need to look to Bud for a cue to reorient and realign my orbit, and it all becomes clear: this may be a voyage into uncharted territory, but we are never in free-fall. We're connected. We're synchronized. And I have never felt more grounded.

Flood Plain

by Bruce Mills

WITH MY FOUR-YEAR-OLD SON, Jacob, I enter the front doors of Croyden Avenue School and move toward the steps that descend to the classroom for children with autism. He lingers at the top of the stairs and, as most days, pauses to look at his reflection in the glass walls. The ritual is not new so I wait, calling his name once or twice out of habit, before directing him down the steps to his room.

After returning to my car, I sometimes enter my own sensory memories of grade school: the sound of stiff new jeans scissoring down corridors, the sharp cries across a playground, the art room odor of crayon, the touch of white paste and papier-mâché, the brilliant reds and purples of thick-textured paintings dried and cracking like late summer creek beds.

I remember walking down to the playground of my Northwest Iowa elementary school, Arctic Cat snowmobile boots tossing fragments of snow from my heels, blackened mittens on my hands, a basketball tucked under my right arm. Alone, I launched shot after shot at a hoop positioned on the end of the asphalt surface in front of the school. Before long, the ball grew slick and harder to balance on the wide mittens. But, in my imagination, I was always a point behind and poised for the miraculous last shot, for some sign that divinity still intervened for those who held out in the cold. When the temperature was well below freezing, I wore a ski mask. On those frigid dusks of mid-winter, the moisture from my breath would dampen the thin cloth, and the cotton would freeze and harden. When the mask rubbed awkwardly against my cheeks, I would take it off and give life back to the frozen cloth by blowing my hot breath through the icy layers. When it grew dark not long after five, I would slowly walk over to the west side of the building, position my forearms on the brick ledge of the window casement, kick my feet against the wall, and balance precariously to see the time on the classroom clock above the cursive alphabet.

I find it odd to have such intimate awareness of this past self, this child who I was that shares no knowledge of who I have become, who comes unexpected and stays only so long as I pause to follow the memory. I watch as he pushes himself back from the wall of the school, bends to embrace the ball, and tightly shuts his eyes to melt the ice that has laced together his long lashes. Hurrying home across the small, snow-covered baseball field, he slides upon a patch of ice and playfully kicks a small drift of snow. Around him, the wind has risen slightly, and the streetlight catches the crystals of scattering snowflakes before they disappear into the shadows. I follow their scattering into the dark before turning the key and driving out of the Croyden parking lot.

Later that afternoon, I wait on a bench outside the front office at Croyden. Jacob climbs the stairs; his hand glides up the rail. He backs into my embrace. As I kneel before him, I gently turn his shoulders until his face is before mine, until I can feel the faint touch of his breath against my lips. "Jacob, what do you say?" He does not raise his chin. "Look at Daddy, Jacob." He lifts his head, but our eyes are like repelling magnets. I raise my hand and hold his chin. He is still learning to see me, to acknowledge my gaze. When he finally fixes his eyes momentarily on mine, it is hard to know whether he apprehends me in a way that I understand. It is a daydreamer's glance, a glimpse of some reverie initiated by my voice. I seem to exist as a memory, not flesh and bone.

"Hi, Daddy." His voice is nourishment, a food that fills me.

Driving home, I ask him if he had a good day. He disregards my question and begins the motif that will become the ritualistic chant of the afternoon.

"Watch TV."

"First lunch and then TV."

"Watch TV. Oh, yeah, watch TV." The "Oh, yeah" is from TV.

"First we eat lunch, then TV," I reply calmly.

"Haveta gonna draw! Haveta gonna draw!"

"Would you like to draw when we get home, Jacob?"

"Haveta gonna draw!"

"When we get home."

When we get home, I draw. I start to sketch in pencil the small Mickey Mouse logo from his *Beauty and the Beast* video box. He watches the ritual acutely; it is always new. He is wary lest I should color the yellow shoes red or the blue hat black. Erase it, he says, when I begin the third Mickey. I have learned to draw gently so that my erasing will not leave marks.

"This one," Jacob says, pointing to the *Walt Disney Productions* lettering. I loop the large "W" and "D" with practiced flourish as my son chants one of the Disney musical motifs. Then he sees something wrong, something that I do not notice. It has to do with the "t" in "Walt."

"This one."

I hear urgency in his voice. I look closely at the letter. I amend.

"This one," he insists. He traces the letter on the table as if I can see on the plastic tablecloth the vivid design in his mind. I watch his fingers; in my palm, his hand would disappear, it seems so small.

"Show me," I say, handing him the pencil. On most days, he refuses. Today, he takes it. He presses hard on the lead and the cross in the "t" slides toward the "D" like a train wreck.

"Oh no, look what you dee-id!" Jacob laments, mixing pronouns and using a phrase and intonation gathered from a Curious George video. Or is it I who he sees as the curious little monkey, creating a mess of things again?

I pick up the pencil and try again and again. Finally, among the scattered drawings that litter the table, I succumb to the frustration, to the seeming emptiness of these unthinking patterns. I toss the pencil down and say "this one" is my "t," that it is the way I will draw the "t," and that Jacob should draw his own "t."

"Draw it!" he replies.

"No, you do it!"

"Daddy do it!"

"No, Jacob do it!"

Suddenly, the papers take to the air, and Jacob runs screaming into the living room. More colors than I can name spread through the room: red and blue and green Duplos clack against the sides of the couch and picture window, the yellow of the box glances off my arm, and the glare of sunlight catches them all, a prism undone. His words break against me, "Want to try again! Want to try again!" In these moments, Jacob will suddenly look directly at me and find the pronouns and names that have fallen off the edges of his sentences. "I want to try again, please Daddy." And I wonder what memory held the syntax of this pleading.

At the end of the week, I again arrive shortly after mid-day to pick up Jacob from Croyden. I sit upon the bench along a wall in the front lobby and lean back against the red brick. Children are arriving for the afternoon. I hear the whir of the elevator of the first bus. From its side emerges a young girl in a wheelchair. Her head tilts against the sparkling plastic head cushion. Her smile unsettles me. She is glancing somewhere where I am not, but I sit up, eager to greet her at the door. I am learning to look into her eyes.

Outside a few flakes of snow begin to suggest themselves, lingering like the descending ash of the burnings of late fall. As I try to make out the snow from the gray sky, another memory urges itself forward. I am twelve and on my Stingray bicycle pedaling through an empty street to a 6:30 a.m. basketball practice. It is mid December. A night snow has covered the street with a blanket of white; except for the shadows cast by the intervals of streetlights and the predictable angles of houses and sidewalks, the landscape has few boundaries. For a moment, I close my eyes and ride blind, until, feeling the thrill of pedaling just beyond some imaginary limit, I stop to look over my shoulder. Behind me, the wandering indentations of my tires, like the frozen paths of small streams, fill with snow, the more distant banks diminished to thin creases of shadow. The street stretches forth like a flood plain fertile with the meanderings of past river channels. It is a world that I had not seen, and so I let myself linger in the space between past and present, this borderless landscape of beauty and loss.

More buses and cars move up to the curb. A few parents enter with their sons or daughters. One child catches my eye; he seems older than the others. After the boy leaves to go down the stairs to his classroom, his mother takes a seat on the other end of my bench. When our eyes meet, I introduce myself and am about to tell her about Jacob just as she is called into the office to talk with the school psychologist. She hesitates a moment, and I sense that she does not want to do the unkindness of not hearing about my son. But I glance toward the office to divert her eyes and assure her. "Perhaps another time," I say.

After she goes, I can feel the vibrations of my son's unuttered name on my tongue and the way my lungs had filled to hold the beginnings of an unformed tale. For a moment, I see myself through her eyes—an eager father whose son now plays in a place previously unimagined and who pauses on the threshold between a world just opening up and another seemingly canceled out. I glimpse with sadness the distinct outlines of that person that Jacob has begun to erase. At first, he remains distant, but I coax the ghost forward with my yearning. Wordlessly, he lifts his head as if in a daydream and meets my gaze. It is not my son's face; it is mine. This lost and wandering self wishes to speak; it cannot, and I find myself gently leaning forward. If I can hold his glance for just a moment, I wonder, perhaps that is enough. And then I think back to the woman's eyes and the healing pause of a hesitant recognition, a shared longing, a hunger for the retelling or a new telling of a story she well knew. It is what we both needed, this amending, this wash of words.

Jacob has had a rough morning, his aide says. He had to have some quiet time because he would not join snack group. During recess, he stood at the top of the Purple Mountain, a favorite climbing toy, and danced on one leg. Even now Jacob is dancing and laughing and saying "Lucky get down! Lucky get down!" Around me I can feel the movement of other children exiting and entering through the sliding glass door.

We walk outside and before I can stop him, he races to the slide at the back of the building, the wind blowing back the hood of his fall jacket. I run after him. He refuses to come with me until I bribe him with the promise of French fries at McDonald's. It takes fifteen more minutes to get to the car. My ears are numb from the cold air; my palms still feel the steel handles of the slide.

Once home, we draw. I search for unmarked paper in the piles of half-done drawings atop the refrigerator and kitchen counter. We have run through the ream of blank paper, so I gather four pieces that promise the easiest erasing and carefully remove half-written words and the limbs of cartoon characters.

"Haveta gonna draw *Walt Disney Productions*," Jacob commands.

I take up the pencil, bracing myself for the fight I see coming. When I get to the "t," Jacob moves off his chair and, clutching the video box, crowds in upon my lap.

"This one. This one." His voice is calm, and I am surprised by how the words seem empty of memory, how the phrases merge together quiet, encouraging, and full of trust.

As I am about to retrace the lines from our previous play, I see something that I had not seen before. Just above the small curve of his pointing finger, barely showing through the dark background behind the lettering, a small loop appears where I thought I had seen a straight cross line. It was never a straight line. It was always a small but clearly discernible loop. With this revelation, I see the smaller letters of the words anew: the way the crossing middle of the "a" touches, but barely touches the initial "W" in "Walt," the way the "s" in "Disney" keeps curling, how the final "y" reflects the hurry of the last letter of any signature. I let the pencil rest for a moment and smell the back of my son's head. I press my lips against his cheek until he lifts his shoulder, leans away, and says, "Haveta gonna draw the 't.'"

Slowly, gently, I press the lead to the page. After I finish, Jacob holds the paper in his hand and, satisfied, lets it fall. It slices the air and then rises for just a moment, suspended, as if hesitating playfully before a final slide to the floor.

When I was young, I would frequently stare out the north window of my house. Beyond the railroad tracks just twenty feet from our garage and not far from the highway running parallel to the tracks spread the flat expanse of a field. I was five and struck with awe at that endless stretch of furrows stitched so seamlessly to the distant horizon, and I stumbled into the question of beginnings. What started all this? What came before the feel of the field upon my eyes, before the dirt itself, before the pulling back of ice and snow? At times, it seems as if I began living that day. The spirit demands the expansiveness of such imaginings.

We walk on vast flood plains. Beneath our feet, the firmness of the ground seems to confirm the permanence of the river channel. To hold up the banks, we press rocks and concrete, believing that our labors can prevent the slide of soil. But there is no telling what may happen when the snow thaws or the next rain comes. The bend in the distance may straighten and, suddenly, the landscape is no longer recognizable.

Living with Jacob is about more than allowing the language of his mind to erase the chalk lines of my own patterns. It is about unexpected intersections, the willingness to walk blind, to discern shadows in the lay of the land. It is about the painful unburdening that comes when the mind expands to see anew.

The Wages of Autism
by Kristina Chew

IT IS A FEW days shy of February 14th. My Intermediate Latin class is working its way through the Roman orator Cicero's first
speech against Lucius Catiline, which—while an intricately crafted
piece of Latin oratory—can be dryer than the driest toast. All of the
students are women and when mention was made of Valentine's Day,
the sighing started.

"I'll be with my friends and we're going to eat fried chicken and
lots of chocolate and . . ." one student announced.

"And a movie. Just not *Sleepless in Seattle*," said another, slump-
ing in her desk. "That would be rubbing it in too much."

When was the time "the romance thing" was the cause of heartache and world-weariness for me, I wondered as one student started
translating a sentence. I am happily married for the past decade and
the mother of a lovely boy. And I answer the question I so hated a
few years ago—"so what grade is your son in?"—without my heart
racing, or any subdued anger. I say: "Charlie has autism. He's in a
self-contained classroom, and he loves it, and he's doing really well."

All of those statements are true, and the three of us have a good
life. And yet.

There are the costs, hidden and obvious—the wages—of autism.

The anthropologist Marcel Mauss has theorized that, in the ex-
changing of a gift, there are three clear obligations: 1) the obligation

to give; 2) the obligation to receive; and 3) the obligation to repay. According to this classification of giving and of exchange, the parent of an autistic child has a lot of 1), while 2) and 3) are big question marks.

Autism is costly in all senses of the word. The psychic and psychological, the emotional and the physical, toll—the ache and the heartbreak—add up and wear parents down fast, not to mention the matter of what it costs, literally, numerically, in terms of doctors' office co-pays and take-out-my-checkbook-and-pay-the-bill. These hidden and evident costs of autism stand out all the more because it is likely that, while we intend for Charlie to have a job when he is an adult, that job is probably not going to be coming with a big paycheck. In the monetary sphere, raising a child with a disability entails giving a lot more than you'll probably receive back from him, and that he'll ever be able to repay, in a dollar sense.

Of course, my husband, Jim, and I would pay two and three and ten times over to help our son Charlie. This boy is worth double his weight in gold and just to hear him say "wait eat fries" is worth a couple of months' salary. If it's affection and love I'm looking for as my Charlie-payback, I reap a goldmine every day. Granted, this is because I have learned to convert Charlie-currency into said affection and love. Charlie can repeat "I love you Dad" and "t'anks, Mommy" clear as day but we often prompt these phrases, especially if we want to hear him say them spoken clearly. Sitting beside my boy on the couch one day, I gave him a big hug and leaned my head into his and I could see the corners of his mouth smiling and he did not move away, and those tiny, almost nongestures were worth a surfeit of gold coins.

The exchange rate in Autismland is more than a bit lopsided. To make these quick currency conversions into Charlie-pence (or kronas, or euros, or rupees, or *ren min bi*), I have had to take several crash courses in a strange and curious economics, a mathematics in which I'm not always sure a point isn't a line or a curve, a physics in which string theory is pretty much proven, and a chemistry in which the Periodic Table reads better backwards, upside-down, and through the looking-glass. I've had to learn a new grammar without my reliable Indo-European declensions and conjugations, a writing system lacking an alphabet or a syllabary or ideograms, and that goes neither left-to-right nor right-to-left, but is total zigzag. The fee alone for this elementary Autismland 101 course has been exorbitant and stretches onto infinity.

And yet, I think, more and more, that this is a fair exchange. Raising a child with autism can really skew more than your perspective on the world, of politics, the cost of living, a peaceful evening. If we put mega-effort and multi-billionaire-Donald Trumpian effort into Charlie's education, so be it. I only know how I melted to hear the clear words he uttered once upon a February evening, a few months shy of his tenth birthday: "Wait eat fries!"

Other memorable phrases that have provided evidence our efforts are paying off:

"Kristy photos, Mommy I want!"

"Kaaaaa. Kaaaaaaaaahhhh!" (Charlie imitating me coughing)

"Mike, yes!" (With sparkling eyes on hearing his ABA therapist would be coming)

"Fold da bankett! Towel on. Care-wots, more care-wots Mommy."

"Water! Cup water. Stayin shower, yes." All to the tune of "Little April Showers" and a bit of "Amazing Grace."

"Giff!" Charlie hands back to me an empty blue bowl, from which he has just eaten a green apple while studying a pile of old photos. In this exchange, "give" means "here it is, Mom"—it being the bowl I had (as it might seem) given to Charlie with more in it (a green apple) than when he returned it to me.

An empty bowl accompanied by spontaneous language.

In Autismland, that's fair trade. That's the gift that—more than any arts and crafts picture frames or snowmen or potted plants a teacher and an aide prompted him to make—Charlie gives us on his own, gold smelted from flesh, sweat, blood, spit, and tears (our own mixed in). Boyfriend-less college freshmen can use Valentine's Day to indulge their sorrows in fried food and chocolate and companionship; we autism parents and autism families need our own Autism Hearts Club.

"Bittersweet" is a word that often sums up life with autism for me; the word encapsulates what I feel when I say "my son has autism." And this is not to imply anything about autism as a "night-mare" or something we strive to "defeat" or to "cure" or to "rescue" or "recover" Charlie from. It is seeing your child hurting himself because he was not born with the neurological make-up to talk as easily as many of us. It is the stare of some six-year-old girl and the too-quick whisper of her mother.

"Bittersweet" is *glukupikron* in ancient Greek—*gluku* being "sweet" and *pikron* "bitter." That's the word the Greek poet Sappho used to describe *eros*, love:

> Eros once again limb-loosener [*lusimelês*] whirls me
> sweetbitter, impossible to fight off, creature stealing up
> [trans. Anne Carson in *Eros the Bittersweet* (1986), LP, fr. 130]

Sappho is talking about love of the Valentine Day's kind, but to me, her words apply equally to life in Autismland. What is my lovely boy Charlie but my heart's delight, "creature stealing up" onto my back or, as very often he does today, to give his dad a hug? I don't need chocolate or champagne, or roses or diamonds, to indulge myself or assuage any ache in heart or mind or soul. An absolutely lovely day with Charlie is our deepest pleasure, our purest joy—why we do what we do—and well worth the stiff entrance fee we paid (not to mention the often pricey monthly dues) for membership in the Autism Hearts Club.

Bitter, and so very sweet.

Proverbs 13:24

by Aileen Murphy

He who spares the rod hates his son. . . .

She called to say we needed to talk
knocked on the front door with one fist
held her Bible in the other
Your three-year-old needs spanking
she smiled
he pushes too much
smaller children in his space
does not play well with others
I gaped, fascinated
having lived in the south for not quite a year

I held the door open with my body
waiting while she gathered her things
She and her husband spanked *their* children
she urged, finger still on a Bible verse
the book closed around it
as she hurried her purse strap over her shoulder

Upstairs, I spied from his doorway
as he lay, face on the floor
brio train cars rolling past his eyes
a tune coming from his chest

One year earlier a priest had said the same
nodding confidently, like I would accept his words
based on his profession, his position
as so many others do, as my mother had
when she spanked my child once
when we were out at a movie

I knew nothing
just to *not add pain* to his curious world
just that he was happy alone
in his sunlit, toy-strewn room
singing alphabet songs
without others pressing into
and popping the bubble of light
around him

No Pity

by Maggie Kast

DAY 1. FOR THE last six months, my developmentally disabled son, Stefan, has been trying to make himself throw up, sticking his slender hand down his throat to the wrist, and he can't tell us why. He knows he shouldn't. He will even tease us with a hand-to-mouth feint, a crafty look in his eyes, but he can't say what compels him. Today we have an early appointment at the GI Clinic of a large, teaching hospital, where he's been under treatment for Crohn's, inflammatory bowel disease, for eight years. I'm apprehensive, knowing he continues to lose weight.

"Hi, Pumpkin," says a nurse. "How are you?"

"Hi," says Stefan. "How you?" He steps forward to shake her hand with a slightly uneven gait, one foot turned out more than the other, then follows her into an examining room. Neatly dressed in summer shorts and a T-shirt, he's thirty-four years old but less than five feet tall and beardless, his hair gelled into little spikes. Suddenly he begins to shiver in a way I've never seen anyone do before: deep, bone-shaking tremors that run through his whole body, and I'm aghast. His gastroenterologist appears in the doorway, takes one look and says, "ER—now." We hustle Stefan, frightened and screaming, into a wheelchair, grab the hands he's trying to put down his throat, and hurry down the hall. The doctor explains as we go that chills called rigors (pronounced rye-gores) are caused by an immune response in which the set point for body temperature in the hypothalamus rises, and the body shivers in an attempt to warm up.

"Can't we go directly to Admissions?" I ask the doc, hoping to avoid the busy, impersonal ER where no one knows or has time to understand Stefan.

"It wouldn't be fast enough," he says, explaining that rigors are a common symptom of septicemia, or blood poisoning, and require immediate treatment. Blood tests soon confirm that diagnosis.

"How do you get septicemia?" I ask an ER nurse as she hurries by our curtained cubicle.

"From infection in any part of the body," she says. "Often from hospitalization." Vaguely I remember hearing about resistant organisms living in hospitals, but I can't stop to think that the help Stefan needs might come bundled with lethal exposure. He's trying hard to put his hand down his throat, and it takes all my strength and concentration to prevent him. We're both scared, and sometimes I think swallowing his hand has become a response to fear in addition to whatever is going on in his stomach. Soon his heart races out of control and an ER doctor comes in and starts massaging his carotid artery, watching the wall, not looking at Stefan.

"I'm not trying to choke you," he says, "I'm just trying to get your heart rate down." I don't understand how this works, and Stefan even less, but he lies fairly still, eyes searching for escape like the eyes of a horse in a fire. His usual patter in the hospital—"Almost finished? Go home soon?"—is oddly absent. The bottom falls out of my stomach and my world as I realize that he's sicker than he's ever been before.

Stefan is the third of our four children and lived at home until he was nineteen. His closest brother, Tom, taught him to walk by connecting a tricycle to a red wagon and riding it around the house, Stefan hanging on the back. In their teens, Tom welcomed Stefan to rock band rehearsals in the basement and rhythmic jams with the guys on the front porch, and Stefan was rapturous, listening and clapping. My husband, Eric, a physician, was devoted to Stefan and protected him from the many unnecessary medical tests that clinics and school systems were eager to perform. When Stefan was seventeen, Eric died, and I had to learn to navigate medical waters myself.

Two years later, Stefan found a full and satisfying life with eleven of his peers at a group home run by an agency called El Valor, not far from me. Round-the-clock staff taught him to shower and dress independently, giving him two daily hours of one-on-one training when he first moved in. Seven years ago, he had emergency surgery for an intestinal abscess, a common complication of Crohn's disease, and was left with a colostomy. The surgeon told me it was not reversible, and neither I nor any other doctor questioned this at the time. El Valor stood loyally by, training each staff member in colostomy care and enabling Stefan to lead a relatively normal life with maximum independence. Days he attended a program rich with music, art, and drama at Esperanza Community Services; weekends El Valor took him and his housemates to malls, movies, picnics, and sports events. Family birthdays, holidays, and occasional weekends he spent with me. He liked to perform simple tasks, like finding the mustard in my crowded refrigerator, and we often visited my mother in central Wisconsin.

About once a year, when his Crohn's flared up, Stefan required hospitalization for intravenous antibiotics and steroids, and then his care reverted to me. Sometimes I succeeded in avoiding the ER by phoning the GI fellow on call and bringing Stefan to the GI Lab, but often there was no choice. Twenty-four hours could pass in the ER before Stefan was sent home or admitted and moved to a floor, and I dreaded the phone calls that signaled the beginning of those long nights.

With each hospitalization and in between, various imaging techniques revealed a shadowy area in Stefan's intestines. His inches-thick medical record details yearly CT scans, intestinal X-rays with barium contrast, and nuclear scans to detect inflammation. Stefan hated the tests, and it broke my heart that he had to endure so much, especially as his Crohn's worsened, and doctors added four-hour, intravenous infusions of Remicade, an immunosuppressant. When Stefan began inducing vomiting, they became more and more convinced that the shadowy area was an obstruction, and we scheduled a surgical consultation.

Shortly before Day 1, Lupe, a staff member at El Valor, brought Stefan to meet with me and an older, well-respected, colorectal surgeon.

"I don't think he has Crohn's," said the surgeon. "I see no evidence of it. We'll remove a section of diseased bowel and reverse the colostomy." Lupe and I were flabbergasted. Could he really do this? How Stefan's life would improve without the constant need for colostomy bag change and clean up! This doctor's white hair, no-nonsense manner, and confidence made him convincing, and he was prepared to search through old hospital records for information on Stefan's previous surgery—all good signs.

Lupe and I looked at each other, breathless. Was it possible that he didn't have Crohn's, after so many years of treatment? The difference between the two doctors seemed melodramatic, almost farcical, and I began calling them Dr. Pessimist and Dr. Optimist in my e-mails to family, thinking of a fable we often told about two children who receive a Christmas gift of horse manure. "All I got was muck," says the pessimist. The optimist says, "I got a little pony, but it ran away." Though I feared surgery, we were all hopeful of cure and even betterment of his life until septicemia changed a well thought-out plan into an urgent rescue operation.

After eight hours in the ER, the staff decides that Stefan should be admitted to intensive care, and a doctor comes down to explain the requirements of that unit. Stefan will need a central line (into a large, centrally located vein), an arterial line (for constant monitoring of blood pressure as well as blood gases), and a urinary catheter. (A patient in the ICU is tied to so many devices it's nearly impossible to use the toilet.) In the unit, Stefan scrambles to climb over the bed rails, nearly succeeding, then bites the back of his hand where a brown callous has formed. He growls and swears rapidly under his breath, revealing a surprising mastery of foul language.

I worry about the loss of his independent-living skills: toileting, dressing, and feeding, as well as his human connections and sense of self, so easily destroyed by the machine-driven life of the ICU.

But not until later do I remember the ER nurse's words and realize that hospitals, especially teaching hospitals like this one, are breeding grounds for resistant organisms, created by the prevalence of serious infections and strong antibiotics. Exposure is increased any time a line, intravenous or otherwise, crosses the skin barrier and creates a highway from a highly contaminated environment to the bloodstream. Though we never discover the cause of Stefan's first septicemia, he now has three new ports of entry for whatever organism lies in wait, and it's only the first day.

Day 4. After three days with nothing by mouth in the ICU, Stefan is moved to Dr. Optimist's surgical floor, starving. "I'm hungry, Ma," he says as I arrive. "*Ven acá.*" His sharp ear has picked up bits of the Spanish spoken by staff at El Valor.

"Here I am," I say. "You can't eat now, but soon. What would you like? Hamburger?" Before he moved to El Valor, Stefan was a cosmopolitan eater and even used chopsticks, always articulate with his fingers, but now he sticks to the all-American diet of the group home.

"Yah, hamburger," he says. "Yessir."

"French fries?"

"Yah, fries. I'm hungry, Ma. I'm hungry." Though circular and repetitive, his speech clearly expresses what he feels. He's wearing the big, spongy boxing gloves the hospital uses to prevent pulling of tubes or putting his hand down his throat, and he calls them "mittens." Though he can easily undo the knots and ties that hold them on, he says, "Mittens?" if he feels the urge to make himself vomit, the same way he says, "Gotta take it, gotta take it," to himself when confronted by pills. But his self-monitoring gives way to impulse in a flash. I leave the room for ten minutes to eat, for I couldn't possibly eat in front of him, and come back to find mittens off, IV line and catheter pulled out, bed wet. A group of surgical residents comes by and palpates his skinny abdomen.

"Does it hurt?" they ask.

"Uh hmm."

"How about this?" Touching his arm, gently.

"Uh hmm."

"Are you nauseated?"

"Uh hmm."

"Hungry?"

"Yah, I'm hungry." This scene is repeated over and over, but Stefan has never been able to report on pain or nausea.

"I don't see why he can't eat," says Dr. Optimist. "Give him a full diet." Dr. Pessimist opposes feeding, but he isn't writing the orders, and I want to believe Dr. Optimist, longing to feed my famished son. Feeding will strengthen Stefan to withstand surgery, even though Pessimist doubts he can tolerate food. So far as I know, they do not confront each other over this, nor do I confront them.

At first, I think it's good they disagree, so discussion and argument can reveal the truth. This turns out to be my first mistake. Though they confer at the start, they are not even once both present with me, and my hope for conference by e-mail turns out to be stupidly naive. Pessimist says he can't type. Their differing views lead not to discussion but to management that ricochets from one pole to another.

So Stefan eats with pleasure, and I am shocked to find forbidden foods on the tray, kernels of corn or tomatoes with seeds, things we've avoided for years, told they could cause mechanical obstructions for people with Crohn's disease. When I question a nurse about this, she says, "We don't have any no-corn diet. We only have clear liquid, full liquid, and full." Stefan eats one or two meals, then loses his appetite and wants to throw up. Usually we prevent him, but he's quick. A minute alone in the shower and his hand disappears down his throat.

Day 8. On my way home from the hospital, I stop by Esperanza, Stefan's day program, where live jazz percolates through the summer evening and barbeque smoke thickens the air. I stroll among the clusters of people eating on the grass, but the festive scene feels unreal and out of place, as though viewed on a small television screen in the middle of a vacant lot. Only Peter and Diana White, parents of Benjamin, Stefan's roommate at El Valor, can know what's in my head and heart. I greet them, relieved by sharing the unspoken, then head for home.

Day 10. Dr. Optimist postpones surgery until Stefan's blood counts improve and he's weaned from steroids. Day 1's urgency fades to hours that accumulate like beads on a string. Along with the surgery, my real life recedes, replaced by the hospital's beige halls, blue gowns, and stagnant air. I don't see Pessimist for a week, and he fails to respond to phone messages and e-mails. Frustrated, I contemplate changing hospitals, but don't know who to call or where to go. Would I find better care elsewhere? I've always believed that most teaching hospitals in the U.S. have access to the same scientific research and resources, and I fear losing my credibility and thus my communication with the docs if they find me fickle, irrational, or histrionic. So I stay put and intervene to save Stefan as much suffering as possible, refusing permission for all but the necessary needles, tubes, and tests, trading permission for information. Tears come at night, making me hate myself for this girly meltdown of anger, when a man would put anger to work.

I know if my husband were alive, he would use his authority and forceful character to demand attention and get second and third opinions, breaking the hospital rules that say only staff physicians can see a patient. I picture him storming into this hospital and raising hell, then despair of even beginning to find my way through the medical tangle alone.

Day 15. Pessimist resurfaces, and we talk about Optimist's hope of reversing the colostomy.

"Eighty-six per cent of patients," says Pessimist, "are happy with their colostomies after one year." I'm outraged, knowing he'll never see Stefan with a bag fallen in a great puddle of feces on the floor, as happened just the day before when the nurses forgot to change it.

"I'm dirty," said Stefan. "I'm sorry."

"It's not your fault," I said, as a nurse threw towels over the puddle and laid Stefan on a bed, where his stoma continued to erupt like a small volcano, covering his abdomen.

Day 18. Weekend. The hospital becomes a warehouse, so I don't even think about doctors or plans. Stefan sits in a chair, legs neatly crossed, so thin now they make two perfectly parallel lines, a pair of pipe cleaners. With him is Nancy, one of several nurse-techs who stay with him when I'm not there. She finds his position adorable and points it out every time he assumes it. I get out the supply of puzzles we've accumulated and line them up on Stefan's tray.

"Which one do you want?" I ask. Stefan points, and I spread out the pieces.

"What's for dinner, Ma?" he asks.

"I think you'll get some broth and Jell-O," I say, "in about two hours."

"I'm hungry," he says. He's an expert at puzzles and keeps his mind on the task, picking up each piece with precise fingers and trying it with each other one, regardless of color or image. I work on the edges and make suggestions, sneaking a peak at the picture on the cover for clues.

"Try this one," I say.

"OK, Ma." We do four puzzles before he tires. I've bought him some new CDs and brought old favorites from home: songs by Pete Seegar, "Satch Plays Fats," a Beatles album, "Bluegrass from Heaven," a Leonard Bernstein compilation that includes "Pomp and Circumstance," and "Soul Hits," very popular with the nurse-techs. He slips a disc in with his usual skill and presses "play." Nancy and I begin to clap and dance to the bouncy, circus rhythm of "Tears of a Clown," by The Miracles.

"Oh yeah," says Stefan, swaying from side to side, roaring and clapping. "I like that."

"You like music?" asks Nancy.

"Yes, I do," he says. "Yes I do."

Day 19. "Go for walk?" asks Stefan as I arrive.

"He's been walking all morning," says the nurse-tech, and this becomes the new routine. Up and down each corridor of the floor and across the no-man's-land that connects East and West, where the service elevators are, pushing his IV pole, with me or one of the sitters. He peeks into a room and gets excited when he sees a young man with shaved head.

"Hi Tom!" he says, so pleased to see his brother, and I explain to the stranger that Tom also has a shaved head.

Day 20. Troops of residents and interns march into the room, make no introductions. They shout a few questions at Stefan, then talk to each other in code. Over and over I find one resident I can talk to and note the name and contact numbers; by the end of the week he or she has rotated into the void. One doesn't speak to people, but services. "I'll ask radiology about that," a doctor might say, or "Nuclear medicine says . . ." I place my hope in the promised surgery, and this is my second and more serious mistake.

Day 23. They open him up and find an inoperable tangle of intestines and mesentery, the blood vessels that supply the gut. They try to biopsy the mass, start runaway bleeding, and close him in less than an hour. At first they call it a Desmoid tumor, a mass that is malignant but noninvasive; later call it simply unknown. Still later, a mesenteric angiogram reveals the mass's structure, but cannot name it. The diagnosis of Crohn's recedes in importance, as Stefan's body refuses to speak the language of medical science.

I begin to doubt he will ever eat normally or return to El Valor, though they are holding his place. I don't know how he will live his life or I, mine. At night I can't sleep and read the "moral essays" of Alan Jacobs. While sitting with a dying friend in a darkened hospital room, Jacobs observes a shiny balloon turn a smiley face to the wall. Reflecting on this apparently trivial symbol, he sees illness as a classical *agon*, dignifying the sign with the agonizing struggle that all will eventually face. Will I find something among these endless halls and days to dignify the unbearable contradiction between Stefan's hunger and inability to eat? Maybe not, but Jacobs's essay comforts by including Stefan's and my personal stories in a universal one.

Waking, I yearn to return to dreams.

Day 30. Following the useless surgery, Stefan is at first heavily sedated, then weak. Nurses who saw him walk before surgery are shocked to see him so passive and debilitated, and nurses who meet him now ask if he's ever been able to walk. Optimist orders full diet again and Stefan, restrained, vomits at night and aspirates, causing pneumonia. Back to intensive care, now on a ventilator. He's learned to bite on the flexible tube to prevent suctioning, and they've responded by adding a rigid, plastic airway. Sedation is wearing off, and he's choking. A respiratory therapist enters. I point out that Stefan needs more sedation or to get off the ventilator, and he says, "I haven't heard anything about pulling a tube." I ask for a doctor and eventually one orders the extubation. "You win," says the respiratory guy. I wonder with horror what happens when *he* wins. Freed of the tube, Stefan says hoarsely but with perfect articulation, each word separate: "I – need – help. I – need – help." I think if he must die, it shouldn't be here.

Friends who live nearby invite me to dinner. The evening is warm, and we sit on the porch above a garden, a luxurious tangle that seems to extend without limit in the setting sun. I am held by their welcome and the care they've taken with the meal, their care of me, for me. We have a glass of wine and tapenade on crackers, as I tell them Stefan's news.

"You seem to be doing all right with this," says my friend.

"That's because I've left the hospital," I say, with a sharp laugh. "I always feel worse in the morning, before I go." This is true, but I hear the rapid clatter of my voice and realize I've taken leave not just of the hospital but of much of my feelings. What happened to Stefan today was unspeakably cruel and heartless. If I let myself feel its full impact, I couldn't go on, and I've instigated what my late husband used to call "martial law." You give yourself orders, and you carry them out.

And you take comfort where you can. Right now, in a classical Pesto Genovese, the basil-and-garlic flavored sauce mixed with spaghetti, potatoes and bright green beans, accompanied by grilled asparagus. Then a platter of red and Green Zebra tomatoes, ripe when green, fresh from the shadowy garden. By candlelight we eat espresso ice cream with raspberries and brownies from a nearby bakery, talking late about Stefan and books and writing and painting in the thick, embracing dark.

Day 35. Back on the floor, Stefan is helped to a chair but can't bear his weight and has difficulty crossing his legs. His fingers tremble when he picks up a puzzle piece, and he lacks the strength to press it in place or to open the cover of a CD player. In bed, he can't center his body or scoot up or down.

Finally I do what I should have done before surgery: ask everyone I can think of for help. A physician friend recommends an aggressive surgeon at a different hospital, willing to take on difficult cases. We meet, and he views Stefan's images on disc. In a month or six weeks he'll chance the risky and exhausting dissection of the mass from the mesenteric blood vessels, something only the bravest and most dedicated would even consider.

Day 50. Stefan says, "I'm hungry" every five minutes for an hour, and my responses are no less repetitive. What can I do?

Day 53. Calling to leave a message for Dr. Optimist, I discover that he is gone. Gone, altogether and permanently. To London, says his secretary, and if he comes back at all, it will only be to tie up loose ends. Stefan and I are not among them. Though I've been told that members of the colorectal team all work together and share patients; though I try to contact them repeatedly and tell Dr. Pessimist how unconscionable I find their behavior; I never meet a single one of the surgeons again. My friends and relatives offer hypotheses. Optimist is merely posing as an M.D., suggests my oldest stepson, a physician; on the lam, say others; a drug deal gone sour; a love affair. He may have been cheery about London or drugs or love, but that had nothing to do with Stefan or me, and I was a fool to be taken in by his mood. I demand a conference with Dr. Pessimist, who points out that Stefan's blood counts must improve before he could survive further surgery, then says, "You know, you're his advocate....if it weren't for you . . ." and trails off. Through his unspoken thought, the silence of the surgeons speaks loud and clear of Stefan's disability and their own distaste for a hopeless case.

I cancel all my appointments and dates; miss a turn I take every day. Little pleasures grow in importance: movies on DVD, the weekly farmer's market. I'm excited out of proportion by discovery of a Vietnamese sandwich shop on my way to the hospital, the drive I dread, and I'm tickled by a Melanesian pidgin expression for the Trinity I hear on the radio: "Na Papa, na Pickininny, na Spooki," repeating it to myself and relishing the whimsical Holy.

I'm beginning to understand what taking care of yourself means. I've always thought it a "me generation" antidote to guilt or excuse for self-indulgence, but now it feels like a triumph of the selfish gene, a biological imperative with a life of its own. Ambivalence has never felt so much like two people inside me, as the pleasure-seeking one elbows its way past mother love and compassion with the willfulness of a two-year-old and a diver's demand for air.

Day 61. Stefan begins working with Kelly, a young physical therapist, who teaches him to use a walker. I time my visits to coincide with hers, though she communicates perfectly with him, because it's so satisfying for me to help with something constructive, to see him make progress, and to have company while doing it. Blonde and cheerful, Kelly coaches him with an ideal blend of demand and patience. The nurse-techs cheer him on. As he gets stronger, he slowly resumes his habitual role as life of the party, chatting after his PT sessions.

"I gotta wife. You gotta wife?"

"No, sweetheart, I gotta husband." Laughter.

"Oh, husband, yeah. Husband. I'm hungry. I gotta girlfriend."

Day 66. The Whites invite me to dinner at RoSal's, a family-run restaurant near the hospital. As I walk there, the blue sky grays, and the incandescent lights of Taylor Street, Chicago's Little Italy, come on, welcoming me. The hospital hasn't retreated, but the embrace I sense is big enough to hold the institution, Stefan, and me as well. The Whites order a round of Prosecco, and I tell them what's up with Stefan. Then Peter asks:

"What do you want to do when you retire?" I haven't thought beyond Stefan for weeks, and now we begin to discuss how to live the last third of one's life. We share a salad and eat rich pasta dishes like ravioli with Gorgonzola sauce, drinking a bottle of wine. Frozen

parts of myself stir and stretch, engaging in conversation ordinary
enough in its content but exalted in its power to revive.

Day 71. I discover that Stefan's blood cultures show VRE, van-
comycin-resistant enterococcus. I barely register the acronym at the
time and don't know what it is, but can't miss the defensive outfits
now worn by those who enter Stefan's room: blue, disposable gowns,
masks, rubber gloves. These precautions are intended to help prevent
spread of the organism, but most of the docs don't observe them, and
neither do I. I ask a resident if there's any cure, and she says, "Once
you've been colonized...." I think of organizing a rebellion or dem-
onstrating for home rule.

Later, research tells me that vancomycin is a powerful antibi-
otic, usually used as a last resort against bacteria resistant to penicillin
and other drugs. First identified in the U.S. in 1989, VRE is spread
by direct contact with body fluids, the hands of health care workers, and environmental surfaces, in addition to lines. Like friendly
fire for the military, this organism is modern medicine's dirty little
secret, the danger you don't hear about until it's too late. The vague
understanding of resistant organisms I had on Day 1 was probably
based on conditions before 1989, and now VRE seems like today's
leprosy. I am outraged that Stefan has become three times untouch-
able: handicapped, inoperable, colonized.

Days 70...75...80...90. How can these days keep accumu-
lating? The hospital doesn't like it any better than Stefan or I. "He
can't still be here when the services rotate," says a social worker. "You
must find him a home by tomorrow." El Valor can't take him on IV
feeding, and "tomorrow" a seizure or pneumonia lands him back in
the ICU.

Day 93. Discharged to a barely adequate nursing home, Stefan
continues physical therapy, always hungry. I work with sitters to re-
store his ability to dress and use the toilet himself. Nine days later, his
temperature rises, and I meet him in the ER at midnight, find him
shaking like a jackhammer and blubbering nonsense, delirious.

Day 102. He's back on the floor in his hospital bed, and I am worn out. Every cell in my body resists return to this place. It's a Saturday, and I resolve to visit for only one hour on my way to dinner with a friend who lives nearby.

"Wha's for brea'fast?" Stefan asks as I enter. I respond as usual by talking to him about food, painting word pictures of cereal, pancakes, or eggs. "I like scrambled," he says. I tell him soon he'll get some broth and Jell-O, and he repeats, "broth, Jell-O," then starts over. "Wha's for brea'fast?" I go to dinner and on to a concert, where I turn off my cell phone, then go home. The flashing red light on my answering machine tells me that while I was breathing fresh air and indulging myself, Stefan's life came to an end.

Then all the days collapse into the time gone by when Stefan lived, and now becomes a strange and out-of-kilter time, my children numbering three instead of four. I walk the still-warm streets, slowly, wanting to go on doing things for Stefan and wondering where the summer went. At first I was glad that they couldn't reach me. They wouldn't have let me get near him, I thought. Later I regretted it deeply, not to have held his hand, at least, as he died. I still do. I grieve that Stefan will have no more music to clap to and Cokes to buy, no more pets to annoy or candies to unwrap and stash in his pocket. I grieve that his innocence will no longer point to the goodness of things as they are. But I'm relieved that he's escaped the trap of hunger and nausea, and do not grieve for myself. Each day I wake and think: *I don't have to go to the hospital today.*

A month later I saw from a charge account bill that day 102 was the day I ordered a pair of flannel pajamas from L.L. Bean, something for fun, just for me. Pajamas, short visit, the meal with my friend, the concert, the turned-off phone: I wish I'd been able to wait one more day before I succumbed to the selfish gene, before I gave in and gulped air. I wish I'd recognized lack of communication as a fatal flaw, and I wish I had not delayed my appeal to friends, the day I said, like Stefan, "I need help." Had I found the alternate surgeon before day 23, saving Stefan's strength for a different surgery, I might have been able to change his fate.

Two months later I received a note from a friend whose son suffers chronic fatigue. She said, "How lucky our children are to have found us as parents." I'd never thought of Stefan as lucky, least of all during his illness, and I was moved by this reversal of priority: not that I gave birth to a handicapped child, but that Stefan existed *a priori* and might have ended up with any parents. The thought was like forgiveness; he could have done worse.

Stefan's funeral was as eloquent as the hospital was incomprehensible. Held at St. Thomas the Apostle, the big church he'd attended while living at home, it was filled with his housemates and staff from El Valor, his out-of-town siblings and their childhood friends, teachers from his day program, and people he'd befriended in the neighborhood as he grew up. My daughter had made a photomontage of Stefan, and his housemates passed it around, touching and feeling him again in his image. "Ooh, it's Stefan," said round-faced Karen, blonde hair in barrettes, dressed in her best. "Let me see," said Kim, with short, black hair, articulate. She gave me a hug. "I have to give you two more," she said, "for my sisters," and she did. "Hi, David," I said, and he looked at me, wordless as usual, in suit and tie.

One hundred and two days of isolation melted in this community's warm embrace. I remembered Dr. Pessimist saying, "If it weren't for you…" and thought *no, if it weren't for his friends and staff, neighbors and siblings, and his six-year-old niece who came to the funeral all the way from California….* This vast network had touched and shaped Stefan's life, as it would for any well-connected person. Though I was his flawed but present companion for those 102 days, these communities had provided so much more for the time of his life.

At the start of the Mass, we invited people to speak. Diana White remembered the strange sounds that used to come from two sides of the church, as Stefan echoed the last lines of prayers, and her Benjamin sang. Subdued rustling and murmurs lay like a carpet under a neighbor's tale of Stefan's trick-or-treating and continued as two teachers sang.

Peace is flowing like a river
Flowing out through you and me

Flowing out into the desert
Setting all the captives free.

"Now?" asked muted voices. "Is it time?" "Should we go?" Then a ragged procession wound its uneven way to the front of the church and back, as each of Stefan's housemates placed a white rose on the coffin, shy or proud, shuffling or striding, until the white drapery was piled high with flowers. The next day two roses accompanied the six-year-old, my granddaughter Iris, back to California, where she showed and told their story to her kindergarten.

After the roses, I stepped up for the Mass's first reading, but people weren't through, and the stories continued. My daughter said she'd intended a plea for Stefan as a person of depth and feeling, not merely sick or handicapped. "You can tell by all of these speakers," she said, "even interrupting the Mass, that people found Stefan uniquely equipped to lead a happy life and to make others happy. I feared that you would remember him as handicapped and sick. I wanted no pity in this celebration, and now I discover I needn't have worried—there's no pity in this room."

Two years before, at my mother's memorial service, Stefan had clapped with rhythmic excitement when a jazz group played her favorite tunes at the end of the service. Of course, a funeral serves only the living, and no music can rouse the dead to dance. Nonetheless, at Stefan's funeral we clapped as well as wept, following the coffin out of the church to the upbeat tune of "This Little Light of Mine," knowing that he would have burst into applause and little yips of joy.

The Stone

by Barbara Crooker

was heavy.
The family carried it
with them, all day.
Not one
could bear
its weight, alone.
Yet how they loved it.
No other stone had
its denseness,
its particular way
of bending the light.
They could not take
the stone
out in public,
had to keep it home,
let it sing songs
in its own strange language,
syllables of schist and shale.
When the mother's back ached,
the father took the stone
for a while, then passed it
from sister to sister.
The stone

became a part of them,
a bit of granite
in the spine,
a shard of calcite
in the heart.
Sometimes
its weight
pressed them
thin, transparent
as wildflowers
left in the dictionary.

Sometimes
it was
lighter
than air.
The stone
did not talk.
But it shone.

PART III

And the Shoes Will Take Us There

As Great As Trees

by Ann Douglas

IAN SAYS GOODBYE TO his classmates on a Wednesday afternoon, three weeks into fifth grade. His classmates present him with a piece of goodbye cake. Conveniently, his birthday has fallen the day before, so they are able to save him a piece of the birthday cake they ended up eating without him—the downside of being suspended from school on your very own birthday. When the decision to suspend him evolves into a request (nonnegotiable) that we withdraw him, the birthday cake morphs into goodbye cake to go.

Everyone stands at the front of the classroom, while I snap a few photos at Ian's request. The teachers and the principal try to smile and pretend to look relaxed, but they come across as awkward and uncomfortable when I look at the photos later on. And as for the kids: they are either glancing sideways at one another and snickering or standing frozen like statues who have been asked to play themselves in some mime version of an ordinary day at school. The boy Ian hit, resulting in his suspension, is standing next to him, making like they're best buddies. Poor kid. He's probably as confused as Ian is, if not more. I'll have to tag this batch of pictures "Theatre of the Absurd."

Getting out of the building isn't as easy as snapping the pictures. By the time I come back for Ian's third load of stuff—how can anyone accumulate three loads of stuff in three weeks of school?—he is crying. Hard. I hug him and guide him out of the school, doing the shuffle-walk that is the only option when you're holding on to someone for dear life.

As we make our final exit, we pass a wall-sized bulletin board gleaming with photos of shiny apples and the smiling faces of every child in the school except my child. I guess he wasn't the right kind of apple.

"There's something different about Ian, but I can't quite put my finger on it." That's Lorrie, his childcare provider, expressing her concerns back when Ian was not even two years of age. She's worried about his language delays and his general "floppiness" (her way of describing his poor muscle tone). She has recommended that we have Ian assessed by the local children's center to see if there is something going on with him—some sort of problem that needs to be addressed.

There is. Phonological processing disorder, for starters, and both small and gross motor delays. I feel that I have to explain to the occupational therapist why I'm crying. I'm worried she'll think I'm a head-case for over-reacting. I feel the need to explain about Laura. You see, before there was Ian, there was Laura, a tiny baby who was stillborn at twenty-six weeks gestation as the result of an umbilical cord knot. Ian was born eleven and a half months after we buried Laura in an unassuming graveyard, between two elementary school playgrounds, near the base of a maple tree.

The experts take their time in coming up with a definitive diagnosis for Ian. For a while, the working diagnosis is attention-deficit disorder (possibly with the hyperactivity piece thrown in). The term oppositional defiant disorder is bantered around, too.

But it isn't until after Ian is asked to leave his school (a common way of safeguarding kids' school records and private schools' reputations) in the Fall of 2007, at the ripe old age of ten, that a second psycho-educational assessment is completed and a diagnosis seems to stick.

Eight years is a long time to wait to get the correct label for your kid and even longer if you're the little boy waiting for someone to solve the puzzle that is your life. It means added days, weeks, months, even years of being teased and tormented, mislabeled and misunderstood; of having your reputation cemented in your neighborhood and at school; of starting to believe that you're bad or defective or crazy—or all of the above—because you've heard people say that about you often enough. It means wondering what there is to look forward to in life when you're not allowed to go to a real school like a normal kid. Things can get that bad.

So let me tell you what we did after Ian was "asked to leave," if you prefer the white-washed euphemism, or, to use Ian's preferred more honest term, "kicked out." We decided to home-school, and spend that time working on undoing those eight years of misunderstanding and confusion.

Our immediate goal was to make him feel good about himself and to convince him that there were things in life to feel happy about, even if the bottom had fallen out of his world. We recruited people to Team Ian and asked for their support over the short-term and the long-term. We let them know that we didn't know what we were dealing with yet, but that Ian could really use their love and support—via phone, e-mail, fax, in-person, *whatever*. He needed reassurance that he was a worthwhile human being and that, once he made it up this side of Horrible Mountain, the world would start to be a fun and interesting place again.

That was the most immediate priority. Then we focused on finding an instructor who could help us home-school Ian out of my office, which is basically a cozy two-bedroom bungalow. We found a fabulous young fellow, Robert, who hopes to attend teacher's college next year, and who has been an absolute gift to our family.

Here's how it all works.

Ian comes to work with me and is home-schooled in the kitchen of the office. Although this around-the-clock togetherness can get a bit intense at times, having a combined home-school, small office (HSSO) is going pretty smoothly, all things considered.

Ian pops into my office at least five to ten times during his school day to give me updates on how his day is going. He might update me on the speed at which he can accomplish a sheet of math or the fascinating or outrageous fact he just read on one of his favorite news websites (he's very political and even more opinionated), or he might ask me if such-and-such a fieldtrip would fit into the family's schedule. He's very good at keeping other people organized.

And then there are the days when he doesn't even have to leave his desk in the kitchen for me to know exactly how his day is going. I can hear the updates live through my office wall.

Robert handles the meltdowns beautifully, but sometimes I sit in my office while the storms are raging on the other side of my wall, wondering how Ian will function in the real world—in high school, when he returns to school; when he grows up and gets a job.

On the good days, it feels like Ian is making huge progress—that in the more relaxed home-school setting, Ian has learned all kinds of ways to manage his frustration without getting stuck in some quagmire of negativity. On the not-so-good days, it's easy to feel that we're back armpit deep in the bog, breathing in the sickening stench of missed cues and missed opportunities: should haves and could haves; false blame and false hope.

On the day of the mini-fridge meltdown, it feels like we've taken a giant step backwards—one that lands us smack-dab in the playground, where typical kid hijinks would be interpreted as a deliberate conspiracy to offend him and infringe on his turf.

Ian turns himself into a human barricade. He's determined to blockade the spot in the newly renovated office kitchen where I intend to move the mini-fridge. "It can't come in the kitchen until Dad moves the plug," he insists, over and over, unwilling to listen to any other possibilities or solutions.

He's so enraged by my insistence that the fridge has to move out of its present—very inconvenient—location that I swear he's going to snap and hit me or Robert, but he doesn't. The fridge is allowed to move to its new home. This is major progress, but I feel like I've been flattened by it in the process.

I retreat to my office and go through the motions of working. I have no work brain left, so I switch into autopilot and start flipping through the photos on my computer. Here's a photo of Ian high amongst the trees. He's about to try the high ropes with some of his friends from his old school. He's standing next to his former principal, wearing a safety harness. The expression on his face tells me he's both determined to give this a go and afraid of where this journey is going to lead.

Here's another. We're up north at the cottage where our family vacations every year, just the two of us, committing one of the cardinal sins of cottaging: Thou Shalt Not Block the Cottage Road. Worse, we're doing it for a totally frivolous reason: we want to stop and gaze at the tops of the trees. Never mind that it's the middle of the week and no one is around: it still feels like we're doing something deliciously, wickedly wrong. That makes it so much more fun. Ian has a huge grin on his face, which I capture as I snap his photo by focusing on my car's rearview mirror. We take some photos of the towering branches of the giant trees arching together over the road, blocking out huge chunks of the almost too-perfect sky. Then we hop back in the car and continue on our journey. We can't let a day like this get away.

An e-mail arrives in my in-box. "How great you are," reads the subject line. It's a poem, from Ian. "Mom, your as great as trees," reads the opening line.

It's a perfectly timed gift, like Ian himself: hope after hopelessness. It's also a reminder that I will always be called to do some variation of this one-two dance with my son. I'll lead and he'll follow; he'll trip and I'll do my best to break his fall; he'll spin around and around and I'll applaud his solo debut, holding back traffic so the world can't spoil the moment.

Other Child, Other Mother

by Cheri Brackett

I WAS STANDING IN a sunny patch of grass beside our blanket in the middle of the north woods of Maine in the month of June. I stood strong in my yoga mountain pose, *tadasana*, eyes closed with my head tilted toward the sun. My husband, Tom, and my fourteen-month-old daughter, Audrey, were sprawled out on the blanket like sleepy cats in a window sill, absorbing the typically delayed warmth of spring.

I turned around to join them and was surprised to see that Audrey had tottered to her feet and had begun to walk away from us and toward the edge of the forest. At the time I was finishing my graduate studies in early childhood development, and quickly identified this as a typical attempt to individuate. Many young children do this at some time or another—they very briefly and without thought wander away. The textbooks would say that she was momentarily dis-identifying with her caretakers and experiencing her first sense of autonomy. I also "knew" this would be a short-lived attempt—she was too tied into us, too identified with us as her protectors to release her attachment for very long. After all, we were "good" parents—attentive and loving, literally racing each other to her crib each morning when we heard her stirring.

I looked at Tom in that knowing, expert way—chin lifted, eyebrows raised. "Watch this!" I said as Audrey wandered farther away from us and into the shadowy woods. "She'll turn around in a few seconds just to make sure we're still here." Seconds became minutes. She never looked back nor did she stop walking. Tom sprang to his feet, and he and I, amused and somewhat bewildered, scurried to catch up with our individuating cherub exploring the dark and unfamiliar places ahead of her.

Many long years have passed since that day, and you can still find us following our now ten-year-old cherub into unknown, unmapped, and oftentimes dark and grievous places. However, today we are much more seasoned and educated in ways that far exceed graduate-level curriculum. Little did we imagine what stamina and skills would be required of us to navigate simple play-dates, ordinary community events, complex psychological/medical evaluations, and entire school systems.

I was standing in the hallway of the University of Maine at Farmington Nursery School. As advised by well-meaning friends, the day after Audrey was born, we placed her name on the school's enrollment waiting list. This was the best child-centered, play-based, early educational program available in the area designed specifically for three- to five-year-olds. It incorporates "creative, individualized curriculum based on developmentally appropriate practice, fosters young children's social, emotional, and cognitive development and introduces them to positive early classroom experiences." This, we decided, was the perfect first school experience for our three-year-old daughter.

And here she was, completing her first day! I was so excited to see her, to hear about her first experiences of engaging with her peers and the most important work at her hands—play. I crossed the room to the water table where she was submerging her toys. I proudly thought how comfortable she looked, that she fit right into the environment. Audrey looked up, saw me approaching and screamed, "NO! NO!!!!!!!!!"

Stunned, I looked around the room, trying to find the cause of Audrey's agitation...only to discover that it was me. As the other children in the room happily united with their parents, Audrey's very vocal pronouncement about our reunion ripped my heart, leaving a wound that Shame and Failure would find as an entry point to my life as a mother. I lost track of the time it took to finally get her out the door, but the room was empty by the time we left. I was beginning to sense something was different with my child, but I didn't know what. We went home immediately afterwards, exhausted.

I was standing in the middle of the community playground in La Jolla, California, drinking in the cool ocean breeze. Audrey, then four, was playing on the monkey bars with her friends, Alice and Isabel. Her play seemed appropriate to me at the time—mostly side by side, lots of imitation, not much verbal reciprocity. Looking back now, I suppose I could have detected that her play activity was somewhat delayed; but she was having fun. I was said to be a "late bloomer," so it didn't concern me if Audrey's skills were a bit delayed or even different. Differences often point to high levels of sensitivity and creativity—characteristics that Tom and I both greatly value. Also, I wasn't, and still am not to this day, a staunch proponent of "appropriate milestone" child development. Each child develops in her own way, at her own pace, and somewhere along the course will catch up or find ways to compensate for skills that may not be as strong as her peers'.

A few other children joined in the play, and for some reason, Audrey took issue with the interruption and change of pace (one of the indications of autism, but also a typical childhood developmental hurdle). She became physically aggressive with one boy in particular (whom I observed to be a bit whiny!) and ended up throwing sand at him. Some hit his face; he cried hysterically.

I had to make a decision whether to let the children "work things out for themselves," or to intervene. I consulted with my friend, Francesca (the mother of Alice and Isabel), and decided to do a little bit of both. I approached Audrey and reminded her of the rules of the playground—mainly kindness and sharing. I also prompted her to say she was sorry to the boy. I know she was listening to me, but I wasn't sure she understood what I said. She often seemed beyond my voice's reach—knowing I was there, but not fully integrating my words. Of course, this speaks to difficulties with sensory integration and auditory processing, which are hallmark indicators of autism. At that time, I just didn't know.

I feel a sense of unease even as I write this, as what happened then so shocked me that I still feel the impact in my body. I looked up and saw a large man, body stiffened with rage, approaching me. Pointing his finger at my face, he shouted, *"You* are the worst parent I've ever seen!" He gathered up his sniffling son and immediately evacuated the park, as though removing them both from risk of exposure to some infectious disease. We went home immediately afterwards, exhausted.

This was the first of many similar encounters—each packaged differently—each containing pronouncements regarding the otherness of my child, creating my otherness as a mother. . . .

"Your daughter has a lot of anger issues," the administrator of the Montessori private school said. "We're concerned about her safety and the safety of the other students and staff. We just don't feel that this is the right placement."

"About the camping trip," my new friend said sheepishly, "some of the other parents have concerns about Audrey being around their children. Maybe it would be best if you all didn't come this time…."

Each encounter, each refusal to include Audrey, fragmented my confidence as a mother. I often found myself alone; fearful I was somehow at fault.

I was standing in the customer service line at a local department store, waiting for what was definitely an inordinate amount of time to exchange an item. I imagined this would be a quick stop before Audrey, then six, and I could go to the children's section and find a book for her. Earlier that year, Audrey had been officially diagnosed as having autism, along with a rare chromosomal anomaly for which there is no name nor any reference to in published research history. Little by little, we had been bringing her into the "mainstream" places in our town—just short jaunts to the grocery store, library, department stores, and restaurants. Tom and I agreed that brief exposure to everyday happenings in our community would help her navigate the storms of stimulation that were sure to occur in public places as she grew up.

Several more minutes passed. The cashier seemed oblivious to the growing impatience of those of us waiting in line, and social mores forbade any of us to confront the cashier personally. What would we say? "I'm wondering if you could be more sensitive to the time constraints of those of us in line. . . ." or "Ma'am, could you please perform your job a little faster?" Or, how about, "LADY WILL YOU HURRY UP!"—which is exactly what Audrey screamed when she reached the limit of her patience. Sensing the wide-eyed gazes and sideways glances from the people in line, my now familiar compatriots Failure and Shame wove tighter and tighter around me like a straightjacket immobilizing me from responding in any way—appropriate or not. Finally, numbly, I explained to Audrey that "Yes, the cashier is taking a long time, but we need to be patient."

"I AM being patient," she screamed, this time throwing her body on the floor. In resolution and surrender, I looked at the women around me and somehow found some words, pleading for some sense of compassion or even understanding of my situation: "Well, that's the beauty of autism…she actually says what we're all thinking." Audrey and I managed to stay in line (which moved a bit faster, I might add), complete our transaction without further incident, and eventually found a book for her to read. We went home immediately afterwards, exhausted.

Being the mother of an "other" child, a child outside the bell curve of "typical" development, places me in the outside margin of that same bell. I am an "other" mother. No matter how hard I try, the skills and milestones I achieve will always fall outside the range of "typically developing motherhood." At times, this continues to be a very painful and isolating experience for me. I also recognize my experience outside this bell curve can't be changed. What I am learning to change is my own perspective and ability to embrace Audrey's unique way of being, even though that uniqueness often leads to great inconvenience, pain, and grief. Ironically, it's in that embracing that I have found wonderful ways to celebrate her and what she brings to this world. I'm able to find new joys and comforts that don't look *anything* like I originally imagined they would.

Audrey is now in the fourth grade. This is her seventh school, four of which asked her (and us) to leave. After ten years of too many doctor consultations and thousands of hours of specialized services, I'm just now able to really experience Audrey's gifts—smack in the middle of the isolation, misunderstandings, even judgments that have entered my life since she passed through my body and into this world. My daughter is a gift who demands that I remain aware of this present moment—in all the awkwardness and frustration, in the rigor of honoring yet managing her presence in the world.

How is being aware of this present moment a gift? In these stories that I've shared, much of the difficulty and heartache comes from a sense of "feeling cheated" or "cast out" from experiences of motherhood that are in the center of that bell curve I referred to earlier. Despite how well-intentioned, prepared, patient, loving, or resourceful I became, I still couldn't yield the results that I hoped for as a mother, according to what I witnessed from other mothers around me. We were all plugging in the same textbook developmental recipes—the "best practices" for raising a healthy, well-rounded, successful child. They were doing the same things I was doing, but they were having a different experience—a better experience, in my estimation. And this is where the gift of present-moment awareness began to change my life.

I started to realize that I was perpetually comparing my experience as a mother to others. That I would long with great sadness to have Audrey follow me like a little chick in the grocery store, or sit snuggly next to me in a bagel shop, or rush to greet me and wrap her arms around my neck after we'd been apart—the way I observed so many other mothers and children behaving. These longings inevitably led to grief, sorrow, and discontent. Gradually, I realized that I wasn't seeing Audrey for who she was, but for who she wasn't—for who I so desperately wanted her to be, and she just couldn't be. I had some decisions to make about how I was going to do this—I could struggle, and continue trying to force square pegs into round holes; or I could let go of these comparisons, and live fully into my own experience.

At the same time, I also recognized that I wasn't acknowledging myself as the valiant and remarkably dedicated mother that I was and am; instead I saw myself as "less than," "not enough," even "never will be." Once I realized how I was dishonoring myself, I saw that I was missing opportunities to appreciate and experience different kinds of connections with Audrey and with myself—connections that other mothers and children may never have. I also saw that my own expectations and comparisons were hindering my ability to really be present to Audrey—to see and be with her as well as to see and be with myself. Realizing this didn't eliminate the grief or isolation, but it did remove it from center stage to somewhere behind the curtain.

Daily, hourly, in each moment that calls for it, I am learning to let go of all these expectations that I held; so many of which were never of my own creation, but were often in alliance with the "normal" cultural standards around me. I am learning to let go of what I expected, imagined, wanted, and felt I deserved—not only as a mother, but as a partner, as a psychotherapist, as a member of this community, as a participant in this human journey. Simply and in surrender, I breathe deeply and pay close attention to that breath. In its rhythm, in that present moment of inhaling and exhaling, I let go of the resistance, the disappointment, the Shame and Failure that creep into my mind and body as the way things "are supposed to be," or should have been. And I once again find myself back in my own life, in my own experience, with my own opportunities (not anyone else's), and present to this very moment—with Audrey, with myself, with my world around me.

It's been said throughout millennia that suffering ("otherness") is a pathway to enlightenment. I'm certainly not saying that having a child with autism has enlightened me or frankly that I'm enlightened at all; rather that I am now more sensitive to opportunities for clarity in my life. Audrey—who she is and is becoming in this world—beckons me to live in this present moment—to live with Presence—with her, with myself, with us. Not in comparison to others, not as I'm doing or thinking something else, but right then, right now. Each time I'm able to relax into this place of Presence I have peace, and a new joyfulness that leaves me increasingly grateful, despite the uncertainty of it all.

I stand in the hallway just outside our bedroom here in our home in Asheville, where we've cultivated a community, a village to surround and support our family. The hall light dimly shines through the doorway and onto the mattress that sidles next to our bed—the space where Audrey now sleeps, and has slept for the past several years of her life. Whether or not this is "appropriate" no longer concerns me, as that concept has lost its relevance and utility in the light of *our* particular family's development. For me it's been rather sweet and quite healing to have Audrey so close at night, needing the reassurance and comfort of her parents in those uncertain dark hours of early morning—so different from those images of her independent self wandering unabashedly and without question into the dark corners of those Maine woods so many years ago.

You can bet that I cherish her need for that kind of reassurance from me; you can also bet that I have personally understood the need for reassurance time and time again in my own life. So, any time I can offer my Audrey a generosity of spirit and reassurance that continues to connect us in positive and loving ways, I do so, without reservation. In this way, both of us receive a great gift.

Of course, there are other stories and gifts to share about Audrey and my experiences with her as her mother. Like when she wakes me up in the middle of the night to tell me she loves me. When she peels herself out from under her covers first thing in the morning and immediately comes to me for a deep pressure hug. When she wants to tell me about something that's happened in her day, even though the words don't quite come together as succinctly as they might, I relish the brightness of her soul in her eyes. When she reads to me out of one of her chapter books (I never thought she'd read!). When she comes to me for comfort because she's confused or angry or has fallen off her bike (I never thought she'd ride a bike!). When she sings—and, oh, can she sing! These moments I especially cherish. They embody connections with her that I never thought would be possible—connections that bypass the otherness of us both.

My "other child" has brought forth from within me an "other mother." What a different kind of journey this has been, and continues to be. Openly and intentionally *living into* this journey invites me to grow into myself in ways I never could have, or ever would have thought to, without Audrey. In a very real way, she has been my teacher—leading me to a sense of awareness and presence that continues to transform my life. For this, for Audrey, in this moment, I am grateful.

100 Percent

by Lesley Quinn

PEOPLE AT THE OFFICE ask innocently enough. Say you are standing in the lobby waiting for an elevator. You are assembled there, a bunch of you, after the finance committee or whatever, in your uncomfortable shoes, budget spreadsheets stuffed inside your zippered leather portfolios, and you start to consider how best to cut your department's operating expenses by the required 5 percent, and you stare straight ahead waiting for the *ding* and the doors to open. To pass the time the person next to you eventually turns to ask politely, "So. How's the family?" and you immediately feel that quickening tightness around your lungs—that gentle, uncomfortable squeeze—and you think, *Here we go*.

You take a breath, a deeper breath than is normal for this elevator lobby. You smile. You nod your head, perhaps a little too vigorously. *All is well in my world*, is what you hope to convey. But what you think is *Please can we not do the parenting check-in thing?*

And yet as you push the elevator's Up button, which is already lit, you turn toward your colleague and immediately launch into an interrogation about his family, his offspring, everything in the world you can think to ask. You remember he has a daughter, and you zero in on her. She graduates this year, right? How were her SAT scores? To which Ivies did she apply? Which is her first choice? What percentage of applicants were accepted there last year, does he know? Is your colleague ready to witness the final, poignant upward stretching of her wings?

People love being interviewed, which is what makes this strategy so effective. But occasionally it fails. Occasionally, someone will manage to parry with one quick question while you pause for oxygen.

Today, your colleague asks, "How's *your* daughter?" You feel a wave of weariness. But you nod quickly. You smile brightly. You say your daughter's name. You say she's eighteen. You glance above the double doors to see where the elevator is now, how many more floors must you wait.

"Eighteen, already? Wow." He will probably ask next where she goes to school.

He does.

You push the elevator's Up button again and make yourself answer matter-of-factly, cheerfully, without hesitation, "A small high school for kids with neurocognitive disorders."

Then you step back.

You wait.

Often—maybe 60 percent of the time—the response to this is, "Oh." Because *neurocognitive* sounds so messy and not fixable, and it always seems to thwart the natural momentum and rhythm of congenial discourse. For people to inquire further, something special is required, something like a straight—yet supple—spine. The remaining 40 percent, those with straight, supple spines, might ask what *neurocognitive* means. Is that some kind of learning disability, like dyslexia?

Your colleague today surprises you; perhaps, after all, he is a superior supple-spine person. At this point you elaborate (briefly, very briefly), that your daughter's school is for kids with one of several brain disorders on the autism spectrum. But there is that word *autism*, and it sounds even scarier than *neurocognitive*, and often after you use it, you can move directly to weekend plans and the weather.

"Ah," your colleague is nodding heartily now. He, too, checks the status of the elevator. He tries to decide if that Up button needs further pressing. "So," he asks finally, "any plans for the weekend?"

But a small percentage—maybe 10 percent—won't be content to stop there. These are the people who will ask how your daughter came to have this disorder. These are the people into whose faces you will look, and if you detect a certain quiet calm in their eyes, you will consider suspending your conversational acrobatics and saying, again without diving into detail, that your daughter had a rough start. You may say (very lightly, very casually and conversationally) that she arrived twelve weeks early, one of those micro-preemies who weighed not quite two pounds.

"But she's okay now?" the optimists will want to know. "Except for the learning disability?" How they long to hear one of those triumph-over-all-odds, happy-ending stories! Here you face another turning point. You will bob your head around in what is mostly a *yes*, with a tiny suggestion of *not exactly*, because by now you are unwilling to minimize, unwilling to construct that simplified, satisfying conclusion. You could, and you don't know why, but now you won't. You just won't do it. Instead, you reward their quiet eyes with that little head-bobbing triangle of truth. *Not exactly*.

You have no need to elaborate. If you can wrap it up comfortably now, and usually you can, you will say something wry and inclusive, something to chase away the small cloud of misfortune, like, "Parenting…always full of surprises."

If yet more is required, which is rare, you will say to the remaining 2 percent, those few with supple spines and quiet eyes and something more—that lovely combination of gravitas and grace resulting from suffering—that your daughter has health issues still, but she is also an incredibly brave and wonderful kid. You smile reassuringly. You thank them for asking. By then, surely, your elevator will have arrived.

But what about the story known by only a tiny percentage—a very privileged few? When your daughter was born you could hold her entire body in the palm of one hand.

Her head was the size of a small nectarine.

She was five months old before you could bring her home from the hospital.

She wears hearing aids.

She adores musicals.

She is a startling mimic.

She has epilepsy and asthma. And periodic panic attacks.

She has long, beautiful blonde hair. She is always asking to dye it black.

She used to have a tumor the size of a large grape behind one eyeball that made it look, until she was about four, like that eye was growing out of her cheek. The tumor, before it was removed, caused the bones on one side of her face to grow differently so her face is—and will always be—asymmetrical, like a cubist painting.

Her teeth don't line up, so it is exhausting for her to chew. To fix this problem her jaw must be taken apart and reassembled.

She is heart-breakingly earnest.

Her laugh, which is the funniest laugh you have ever heard in your life, is famous in your community. Once, at the movies, she burst into her staccato hysterics, and, you learned later, friends sitting elsewhere in the dark theater turned to each other and whispered her name.

Her eyes are a warm brown.

Her skin is very pale.

There are large blue veins running up the inside of her left arm, fanning out from her shoulder across her small, bony chest.

Her hands are tiny, but her fingers are very long. She has nice fingernails when she doesn't chew her cuticles.

The simplest math is impossible for her brain to grasp. It takes about thirty seconds, with her eyes squeezed closed and her lips moving silently and her beautiful fingers outstretched, to figure twenty minus ten.

She has breasts.

She is indifferent to most food (she is four-foot-nine and weighs seventy-eight pounds; at eighteen, she has reached her adult size). Oddly, she adores clams and escargot.

For her, impassive faces and figurative language and certain tones of voice are indecipherable. "Today a boy at school said I looked hot. Was that flirting or was that about temperature?" Or, "Right after Mr. Enholm yells 'Quiet!' in math class, he *smiles* at us. Is he angry? Or is he joking? Or is he joking *and* angry?"

She may not know how others are feeling, but she always knows precisely how *she* is feeling. And she usually knows precisely why.

"Please don't give me unpleasant advice before school, Mom. It makes me feel mixed up and the opposite of cheerful and it ruins my day."

She has recently been experimenting with ferocity. "Excuse me, Dad!" She leans forward at the dinner table, glaring, pointing her forefinger into his face. "Excuse me. You interrupted me. Which was inappropriate because I am the one who is talking right now. Not you." It is hard not to find this funny.

She takes enormous pleasure in recounting, repeatedly and in word-perfect dialogue, long scenes from movies. She is desperate to relive these scenes out loud, and she is often wild-eyed with the inability to keep herself from sharing them…again…and again. It seems impossible for her to remember, or it seems not to matter, that everyone finds this tedious.

Any mention of the word *annoying* in relation to her behavior triggers in her a deep and frustrated despair.

Because she can be someone else for an entire day, she can't wait for Halloween. She begins planning her next costume in early November, and every year decides she will dress up for only one more year. She said this at fifteen…sixteen…seventeen. After *next* year, she says, she will be too old and will stop for sure.

She types so fast her fingers are a blur on the keyboard, and she aches for a boyfriend and worries that no one will ever really love her that way, and she lies badly and infrequently, and once she sees a word on the page, she will never, ever misspell it, and she loves to snuggle, and she loves spending time alone with her laptop in her room (which she keeps perfectly clean and orderly and just so), and she loves Friday nights when she is free from school and free from chores and free from the hard reality of being *her* out in the world, and she devotes herself endlessly to a large and ever-changing cast of instant-message, role-playing, virtual friends whom she adores, and she wishes she didn't have to buy her shoes from the kids' department, and she loves listening to movie soundtracks over and over again, and she loves dogs, and she is, in her heroic little body, a huge presence in your hurting and grateful heart, and for 100 percent of her eighteen years, she has been your biggest and most complicated blessing.

These are not things you can say while you wait for an elevator.

Navigating Autism

by Christine Stephan

OUR FAMILY'S TRAJECTORY SINCE we learned our first-born son Oliver had autism has been both an angle and an arc.

The forty-five degree angle belongs to my Oliver. In the beginning when we sat at that long table surrounded by experts listing our son's many deficits and hearing the word autism for the first time, we were desperate for answers. We felt bombarded with *information*, yet we had no idea what he might be able to achieve in life. No one was able or willing to give us a prognosis. When he was three, we could already see how different he was from other children his age. But would this gap widen as he grew older? Would we have to teach him every-thing? What would age and maturity yield? What would he be able to accomplish in life? Sadly, never once did I think to look at the first three years of Oliver's growth and development as any kind of indica-tion for what I could expect. Never once did anyone encourage me to consider his capacity to learn, evident in the tremendous amount of growth that had already taken place in his young life. Never once did I stop to remind myself of the lovely little *person* he had grown to be. Oliver had autism now; our perspectives had all shifted.

The arc of development is mine. When Oliver was still an in-fant and toddler there was never any doubt—any question, even—that I was the expert on my child. I never would have thought to ask anyone for input on my parenting. I am a believer in attachment parenting and that's what I did: I breastfed him until *he* chose to stop at two and a half, he never slept anywhere but with me until he was ready to move to his own bed, and I carried him close to my heart in a sling until he grew too heavy. I never let him cry without attending to him. I wanted him to feel secure, attached, and not alone in this world. That was the best way, I thought, to help him feel confident enough to develop independence. I never would have thought that someone understood Oliver better than I.

After the diagnosis, my grasp on motherhood, already shaky from the intuitive knowledge that I somehow wasn't fully meeting Oliver's needs, loosened. Or perhaps it became undone altogether. All of the difficult parenting issues that we had faced up until this point suddenly became *pathological.* It wasn't his personality that made him so incredibly stubborn; it was the *autism.* It wasn't that I had not been fully equipped with the information that I needed to parent Oliver well; it was the *autism.* Suddenly there were others (psychologists, social workers, teachers, therapists) who claimed to understand Oliver, who could help us navigate life with this little boy of ours more successfully.

In the wake of the diagnosis, I found myself leaning heavily on the advice of those professionals. During a time when I felt un-moored and lost, it became easy to turn to people who spoke with such confidence. And yet, I now see how much our parenting strate-gies changed, the dynamics in our house shifted; we were parenting by committee. I see how vulnerable we all were and how we lost something intangible and yet so valuable. Here I was, a mother who had carried my child in a sling for his first year of life so that he could feel and hear my heart beating as he had in the womb, and I had somehow agreed to let him "work" with therapists for thirty-five hours per week, shut away from his family and our daily activities. The trust and attachment that I had worked so hard to foster since his birth had lost its priority to all things in service of the autism. Over a period of just a few months we had lost whatever remaining grip we had on our feelings of competency as Oliver's parents.

When the team of therapists first came to work with Oliver, they asked for our input in prioritizing their efforts and wanted to know what we would most like for him to be able to do. With all of his developmental delays, they were probably shocked when we told them that it was very important to us for Oliver to learn to peddle a bicycle. As a family we often rode our bikes together, and more than anything we wanted him to be a part of that. Oliver's diagnosis had caused us to let go of so many hopes and dreams, but we were holding fast to this one thing: that we would all someday bicycle together. I'll never forget the looks that those therapists silently traded with each other, as if to say that we didn't have our priorities straight. Then they delicately explained that learning to peddle could be something we approached during our "down time."

It took months and months for Oliver to learn to peddle. Every day we tried, and every day Oliver just sat there on the bike. Fall became winter and winter hinted at spring and we made no progress. Oliver never objected to sitting on the bike, but day after day he never moved a muscle. Then, one day he just did it—he sat down on the bike and peddled right across our front porch. Now I see what a spectacular amount of physical coordination goes into something like peddling a bicycle, and although Oliver was motionless, it didn't mean that there was no movement. In his own way he was working out this challenge that we had set for him. His work just wasn't visible to us. Our hours of persistence turned out to be about more than just learning how to peddle a bicycle. Holding onto, and achieving, this one vision of life for our family became the catalyst for us to begin plotting a new map for the future; one that drew heavily on our own arcs and angles.

We began researching and finally embraced a family systems approach to autism remediation, Relationship Development Intervention (RDI®), that was more in line with how we had approached parenting before autism became the guiding principle. RDI is a cognitive and developmental approach to remediation that works through empowerment: the parents are given the knowledge and the tools to help their own child. The strength in the approach comes from the bonds of trust and love that were established from the very moment of birth.

With RDI, I again learned to put my relationship with Oliver first and to believe that he will go as far in life as he is able. It is my job to see no limits, only potential. The experts, those who label and classify him, don't know as much as I do about this little boy named Oliver. Because he is not apart from us, his family; he is a part of us. And that realization continues to guide us and the decisions we make every step of the way. It took me two years to reclaim my hold on motherhood, to fully embrace my instinct and intuition again, the arc wonderfully bringing me back to where I started.

Even so, with all the growth and development that gives me such joy, I have struggled with acceptance. I have had a hard time looking too far down the road. The draft of our Last Will and Testament that we had revised upon our second son Sami's birth, and that we retrieved from the lawyer's office three days before Oliver's diagnosis, still sits unopened to this day. Part of me has wanted to believe that someday we will look back and laugh at how much we worried that Oliver would never learn to communicate. Or at how much we worried, period. Because no matter how much I would like to banish it, the worry is still there. Without even realizing it, part of me has been waiting and hoping for a time when things will be different.

I love adventure but I hate being lost. I've often thought of what Columbus knew while navigating the sea: the sun rises in the east and sets in the west. How many times had I gotten my bearings by relying on that early lesson? But when you look at this truism more closely, you'll find that there is more to it than finding simple directions on a compass. If there is one thing that I now know for sure, if there is one single lesson that I have learned in the past two years of parenting my son Oliver, it's this: elementary school teachers and Ernest Hemingway got it wrong. The sun *never* rises. We go round and round.

None of us are standing still even when it seems that we are. We are all making a journey through time and space that literally changes our perspectives and enables us to see the sun every morning. The danger is in forgetting that it is *we* who are moving and not the sun. The danger is in waiting and watching the horizon for a time when things will be different because then we will fail to realize that it is *our* journey that we are navigating.

So it has been with my journey through motherhood. In all this time I haven't really understood that, just like Oliver learning to ride a bicycle, I've been moving even when it seemed that I wasn't going anywhere. One day I woke up and found that his angle and my arc plotted together, give our family a map for a journey that Columbus would envy.

Driving Down the Road... and Growing Up with My Asperger's Child

by Susan T. Layug

SOMETIMES I THINK MY child teaches me more than I teach him.

I have a child who is autistic—mildly—but autistic. He looks like any seven-year-old kid, seems to act like one, and is able to spell words such as "space," "world," etc., like most of them. He loves SpongeBob Squarepants, has this obsession with Lego toys, thinks that boys rule. But if you observe closely, he doesn't fit in this extrovert-oriented world. He barely knows how other people feel or think or whether they're being unkind to him. In other words, he is what kids clueless to his condition call "clueless." To the experts, he has what is called Asperger's syndrome.

Asperger's syndrome is a form of autism where the child's main disability lies in his social deficiencies. By the age of seven, most children know how to strike up a conversation or answer a simple "How're you doing?" "What's up?" or "Do you want to play with me?" To the Asperger's child, the ease of striking up such conversations seems almost unattainable. For example, upon meeting a new acquaintance, the child might talk about an interest such as the city train routes and schedules, rather than ask if the other child would like to play tag. My son once started singing "The Star-Spangled Banner" upon being introduced to a potential playmate.

As a mother of a "clueless" kid, I have to be painfully aware of such deficiencies so as to teach him how to act as close to normal as possible. I have to rehearse social situations with him, prod him to initiate play, and rehearse with him how a seven-year-old makes friends. First ask the other kid's name. When seeing someone familiar, say "How're you doing?" Talk about their pet if they mention it rather than your own Lego Junkbot. In other words, I have to teach him what we, ordinary people, take for granted as part of our everyday social lives.

And yet, in these teaching moments, I learn as much from him as he does from me.

Mothering an Asperger's child has finally helped me build some character— which, up until I became a special-needs parent had been an elusive, if not impossible, exercise of will. I used to be noncommittal. Never got married, never bought a house, never even kept an aloe vera plant long enough to experience its so-called healing properties. But upon learning, and accepting, that my kid has Asperger's syndrome, I no longer had an excuse for this lack of commitment. If the child were to thrive, I had to grow up: let go of my wanderlust, of my will-o-the-wisp-ness, of my improvised jazz rhythm of life. I had to mind schedules, lists of tasks, "cheat sheets" of socially acceptable conversations that my kid has to learn and abide by. I had no choice but to become a better person.

As a creative person, I used to take my spurts of inspiration and my seemingly limitless time to pursue my ideas for granted. Now as a mother of a special needs kid, I value every creative and productive moment I have, be it the time to write this essay or to find the simplest words to explain "suffering," "affliction," or "empathy" to my Asperger's child.

An Asperger's child tends to take things literally. My son sometimes interprets the most naive, and oftentimes wisest, meaning of a phrase. One time as we were driving home, I asked myself aloud, "What am I doing [with my life, that is]?" His response: "You're driving down the road, Mommy." Talk about the here and now, the importance of being in the moment, of putting above all else what is truly important.

In teaching empathy to my son, I learn to be empathetic myself. I no longer smirk at the Asperger's-like employee who makes his rounds making sure all the medical personnel wear their scrubs. I discreetly put on the counter the extra cents that an adult with Down syndrome needs to buy her McDonald's burger. I pause in a moment of impatience to remind myself that, perhaps, the person on the other end of the line is "clueless" as to how to sound friendly and nice, but nevertheless tries his darnedest. I do these things because I now know that special-needs children—and adults—are special gifts that make the human race become more humane.

I am learning to be patient—even to be patient with my lack of patience. In due time, I tell myself, somehow he will get it "right"—if only to be interested enough in making friends and keeping them, if only to forge a connection with a world full of people who need other people. Just the other day in the playground, he asked a girl if she was going home yet. She said "no." To which my son quipped, "Let's play then!"

I am learning to celebrate every little success.

Heart-Shaped Rock

by Kyra Anderson

MY SON FLUFFY AND I went to the beach this afternoon. The sand was warm under the streaming sun as it stretched out to hold the Narragansett Bay in the damp crook of its elbow. The summer crowds had not yet descended and so we camped in a lazy and scattered way, our shoes tossed off one and then the other, our toys spilling out of the crochet sack by the lip of the sinking wave.

A mother and daughter we met on the beach last year arrived by chance. The girl ran to Fluffy, inviting him to make turnovers in the sand. Fluffy was momentarily intrigued and followed her to a freshly dug hole filled with salt water. He looked blankly down and seeing nothing edible, returned to his solitary game of pushing dry sand over mounds of wet sand, his hands splayed like reindeer antlers, his soundtrack one of flying missiles and exploding bombs.

The mother sat down with me. I learned her daughter is completing her first year at a private preschool where they don't tolerate coloring outside the lines. She began the year scribbling wildly across and page and now, *thankfully,* her cheerful suns and flowers remain within the pre-set, bold parameters.

I said nothing.

I thought of Fluffy's crayon battle enactments, the only drawing he does, and how thrilling I find their tangled glory after two years of his refusal to write or draw anything at all.

Soon, the mother's friend arrived and the daughter eagerly skipped beside them on their hike to the northernmost end of the beach where a river meets the waves in swirls and eddies as it tries to push back the tide.

Fluffy continued his game as my husband, Dave, arrived. In a fit of uncharacteristic recklessness, he had purchased an electronic hair buzzer and mowed off his hair that afternoon without so much as a cursory glance at the instructions. There were gullies and ridges, hair jutting behind his ears in pointy half-moons. He was grinning wildly as he approached as if headed toward his parole officer, concocting an excuse for his latest infraction.

Fluffy looked up at him and said, "Who are you?"

The beach was glorious, *like a tonic,* a friend of mine would have remarked. We stayed and stayed and when we got hungry I fetched pizza that we ate on our blanket as a woman in a yellow bathing cap swam parallel laps a hundred feet from the water's edge.

When it was time to go, Dave and I gathered our things, leaving the bagged sand toys next to Fluffy's shoes for him to carry.

Time to go, I called to our son who was running after seagulls, tossing handfuls of sand and small pebbles at their retreating dangling feet.

"Eating dysregulates him," Dave said.

"Do you think it was the cheese?" I said, looking up at the sky.

"The sun dysregulates him," Dave offered, helpfully.

"I wish someone would fly down and tell me what the hell I should feed him," I said, tracking Fluffy as he screamed across the sand.

"Air dysregulates him," Dave said, now to no one in particular.

"Time to go!" I called again.

We waited for him to notice. And waited and called and waited. We were almost to the ramp leading toward the parking lot when he looked up from his position on all fours, swimming through the top layers of sand. We motioned toward the bag and he jumped up to run off in that direction but dropped back to all fours within seconds.

"I tell you, this is basic stuff," I said. "He ought to be coming along with us."

"Kids need to run around, blow off some steam," Dave said.

"I know, but he's not even checking to see where we are!" I said.

We waited. We watched. He was slowly sweeping circles in the sand, *totally absorbed,* I thought, shaking my head, *tuning us out.* I started walking up the ramp, still watching. Finally he looked up and raced toward us, holding something in his hand. We pointed to the bag. He ran back, got the bag, put on his shoes and tromped to where we stood.

"Mommy! Did you wonder what I was doing? Why I was taking so long? Well! *First* I was throwing sand at the seagulls and *then* I was throwing rocks at them and *then* I got the idea to look for a rock! A special rock to take home and THEN I thought of finding a rock for *you!* A heart-shaped rock for your rock collection because I know you *love* them and then I found this one and it isn't *exactly* a heart but it's *almost* one and here it is!"

I took that heart-shaped rock in my hand and my beautiful boy in my arms and strode to the car with my dangerous ex-con husband.

If we were being filmed by an overhead camera and if that overhead camera were to pan out and back far enough so we were just mere specks on the landscape, we would see we are all on a path. Sometimes it winds through parched fields, hilltops, murky waters, dense forest, tall grass, and sometimes the land is verdant and vast, the view majestic, like the earth upon which Julie Andrews twirled at the beginning of *The Sound of Music.*

Of course, I didn't invent this way of looking at life but I find comfort in the metaphor because when I am feeling dark, my mind is about as sophisticated as a cat on a car trip, the cat of my childhood perched on a carload of gear at the start of our family vacation. He couldn't remember the life he had left or the life he was moving toward. He couldn't imagine the Maine for which we were bound and all its pine-tipped splendor, the way the sun punctured early morning darkness and shimmered on the steel gray mud flats, couldn't conjure up the stiff weeds beckoning to be brushed, the grasshoppers waiting to be captured, eaten, and regurgitated.

His life was a bumpy car ride. The end.

I am not a cat but when I am in the tall grass, I forget and it's like this: my life has always been and will always be this vomitous, jiggly journey, trapped inside this car, looking through the slippery windows at things speeding by too quickly to recognize.

When I became a mother there was an instant change that was miraculous! Lovely! Fragile! Everything turned inside out in the best possible way because of this arrival, this *life*. Upheaval! Disorder! Sleeplessness! I stumbled around in my maternity pants and nothing on top, my gigantic breasts on display for every delivery person who arrived with congratulatory gifts and flowers. It was deep winter in the northeast and I was floating in a bubble of zero modesty that began during delivery and ended about three weeks postpartum. There's even a little footage of me doing an African dance with foot stomping and harvest hands reaching down to earth and up to the gods in my PJ bottoms and a stained once-white cooking apron, pendulous breasts flopping about. I look like a lunatic butcher.

The instant change was fine. As the months and years have passed, the gradual change is something I'm still trying to integrate. My tiny pink infant turned colicky at two weeks, screamed for months, and then calmed enough to finally sleep but only when velcroed to my body. At three, he got kicked out of preschool and soon after was diagnosed with Asperger's syndrome. We started to homeschool, selected therapies from the lazy Susan of treatments, opting for the developmental approach—a kind of Respect, Join, and Challenge triumvirate with a smattering of Occupational Therapy and a side of good nutrition. We climbed out of the crisis of *something's terribly wrong* to a place where some things were simply *different*. Not better. Not worse. Harder sometimes, yes. But mostly, just different.

Yet, I'm lonely for the company of grown ups. I'm out of condition, socially, on this stretch of the path. I forget to modulate my voice or to use my voice at all. I laugh inappropriately. I stand too close, like my childhood friend, Joan, who'd routinely careen into me like one of the Three Stooges any time I took a few independent steps. I'm in-between selves, the one I was and the one I'm becoming, hovering like a word insert in a line edit waiting to drop down.

Tonight at bedtime, after a blaster bath to strip his body of sunscreen, salt, and sand, Fluffy solemnly placed the new rock in my ceramic bowl of odd-shaped hearts.

"Oh, Mom," he sighed. "I'm growing up."

"Yes, honey. You are."

I don't, anymore, subscribe to the notion of social developmental age. Fluffy is six and a half. Although he may be closer to two when it comes to his ability to keep up with the rapid exchanges in peer play, he was born six and a half years ago on a cold February afternoon and that will always be true. His mind is complicated, like all of ours. He does math like a ten-year-old, shares his toys like a one-year-old, and dances like his dad.

There's a lot I don't buy anymore. What looks like withdrawing in a child with autism to me is more about shifting for a better view. Fluffy has taken to climbing back and forth under the table of a booth in a restaurant. I let him. Sometimes he stays under there for a while. Some might say he's protecting against sensory input and that may be, but the other day he offered up, *I like to go under the table so I can watch the other people.*

I don't buy that those with autism lack Theory of Mind (ToM), that they can't see from another person's perspective, understand that you may have other thoughts, view, understandings than they have. It may be the case in *some* of those on the spectrum, but I bet for a vast majority it's more of an energy issue. If your energy is used up trying to regulate your central nervous system, you don't have any left over to dip into your ToM pocket and wonder what the other guy is thinking. It's not that you can't; it's a matter of priorities, of the hierarchy of needs.

I don't believe any of the IQ tests results for a child with what is called low functioning autism. How can you believe the scores? It's like testing for cognitive function in a foreign language. I think IQ tests should be banned. Are they really helping anyone? If someone tells me that my son's scores are off the charts, should I slap the flour from my hands and sing out, *All done! Look! His verbal reasoning is through the roof!* Should those who are told their child is mentally retarded throw in the towel? *Forget it, he'll never understand!* The tests provide no real information for how to proceed with what's important in this world: to feel safe, to belong, to be valued, to make a contribution.

Our kids are astoundingly capable. Does that mean they are all geniuses? No. And yes. *Human beings* are astoundingly capable. It's not a matter of how many words we have or the value of our IQ score or even what we, up until this moment, have done. It's all a matter of how well the rest of us see, because real seeing is about tuning in to what is happening now as we turn our gaze to what hasn't yet happened, what is on the way.

After stories and lights out, Fluffy leaned against me in the darkness of his room and stared up at his glow-stars on the ceiling.

"What did you *first* think, Mom?"

"Hmm?"

"Today, at the beach?"

"Well, that you didn't want to leave."

"I didn't."

"I know."

"I was *trying* to leave but when I thought of that rock somewhere under the sand, I *couldn't* leave until I found it."

"I'm glad. I love that rock."

"Oh, Mom. I was hoping you'd say that."

You're Adopting Whom?

by Ralph James Savarese

"WHY WOULD ANYONE ADOPT a badly abused, autistic six-year-old from foster care?"

So my wife and I were asked at the outset of our adoption-as-a-first-resort adventure. It was a reasonable question in this age of narrow self-concern—far more reasonable, or at least more reasonably put, than many of the other questions we fielded.

For example, "Why don't you have your own children?" a wealthy relative inquired, as if natural family-making were a kind of gated community it was best never to abandon. "You two have such good genes," she added. "Why waste them?"

A colleague at work confronted me in the mailroom with this memorable gem: "Have you tried in vitro?" She feared that we hadn't availed ourselves of the many wondrous technologies that rescue infertile couples. "Wouldn't that be better than adopting a child with a disability?" she asked, drawing out the word "disability." "God knows what that kid's parents were doing when they conceived him."

"We're not infertile," I barked. "We have a relationship with the boy."

My wife, an autism expert, had offered her services to the boy's mother, but as the woman found it increasingly difficult to care for her son and then dropped out of the picture altogether, we'd started spending time with him. His first communicative act with language, at age three—the sign for "more"—we'd taught him while tickling his belly.

He later made that sign in the emergency room of a hospital where he was brought after being beaten in foster care. Upon seeing us—we'd been called in to try to calm him—he stopped in his tracks, paused (as if to allow some associative chain to complete itself), and demanded obsessively to be tickled. I remember searching on his chest for unbruised patches among the purple, blue, and black. He was that frantic in his quest for the familiar, and, dare I say, for love.

To this day, I can't believe how callous people were; the strange anxiety that adopting a child with a disability provoked. And the anxiety just kept coming. "Healthy white infants must be tough to get," a neighbor commented. No paragons of racial sensitivity, we were nevertheless appalled by the idea that we'd do anything to avoid adopting, say, a black child or a Latino one.

As offensive was the assumption that we must be devout Christians: hyperbolic, designated do-gooders with a joint eye firmly on some final prize. "God's reserving a special place for you," we heard on more than one occasion, as if our son deserved pity and we were allowed neither our flaws nor a different understanding of social commitment. The journalist Adam Pertman, in his otherwise excellent book, *Adoption Nation,* reproduces this logic exactly when he speaks of "children so challenging that *only the most saintly among us* [my italics] would think of tackling their behavioral and physical problems."

Despite the stigma attached to "special-needs children," people do adopt these kids. And yet, many more Americans spend gobs of money on fertility treatments or travel to foreign countries to find their perfect little bundles. I'm haunted by something my son wrote after we taught him how to read and type on a computer: "I want you to be proud of me. I dream of that because in foster care I had no one." How many kids lie in bed at night and think something similar?

The physical and behavioral problems have been significant, at times even crushing. The last eight years have been devoted almost exclusively to my son's welfare: literacy training, occupational therapy, relationship building, counseling for post-traumatic stress—the list goes on and on. But what strides he has made.

The boy who was still in diapers and said to be retarded when he came to live with us is now a straight-A student at our local middle school. He's literally rewriting the common scripts of autism and "attachment disorder" (the broad diagnosis for the problems of abandoned and traumatized kids). These are hopeless scripts, unforgiving scripts in which the child can't give back.

My son does, and others can as well. Recently, in response to my hip replacement, he typed on his computer, "I'm nervous because Dad has not brought me braces [his word for crutches]." I was just home from the hospital—wobbly, a bit depressed, in pain. To my question, "Why do you need crutches?" he responded endearingly, "You know how I like to be just like you." My son was trying to make me feel better, taking on my impairment, limping with me.

Oh, the Community

by Veronika Hill

I THOUGHT HE AND I were alone when I parked, but then I saw you in the car next to ours. You were a mother just like me, walking the same path, only wearing different shoes. You were all the mothers who have walked that path before us and who will someday walk that path when we are gone.

You and I gathered our things in stereo and I felt like I was looking in a mirror when I noticed your son in his car seat. He was about the same age as mine, maybe four, and it's rare to see another mom and her four-year-old out on a weekday when preschool is in session. I thought for a moment that you might be phantoms.

I saw you again as he and I sat near the fountains sharing grapes and a bagel. You were sitting with your boy a few tables away, and I wondered if you were enjoying the crisp fall morning as much as I was. I wondered if you felt as lucky as I did to be having breakfast with your child.

I fantasized for a moment about connecting with you, about sharing the cool air and sunshine with you. I watched a grackle puffing her feathers, waiting for a crumb. Then I looked up and there were two of you, two mothers, mirror images of each other. That space under the oaks had become a meeting place for you, but for me it remained a place to watch and wonder.

He and I continued to divide and devour our snacks, and you continued to multiply. There were two of you, then four, then six—

all mothers, all reflections of each other. You were no longer a reflection of me. You had become a memory—a snapshot of my past. I thought about the days when I was trying to create a community just like yours, when playgroups were my world. But I was never able to figure out a way to fit, so I abandoned you, the memory, back then.

As I had in the past, today I watched your older children running in circles, and your babies watched me. I was participating silently. I was invisible. I studied you, curiously, as you exchanged smiles and niceties. I noticed a perfect curve in a single lock of your hair. I basked in the radiance of your healthy, glowing skin. I tried to imagine what you were feeling when you dressed your baby in those colorful polka dots that morning. I wondered about your secrets, and I tried to catch glimpses of them on your faces. I hoped you wouldn't look back at me because I didn't want you to catch any glimpses of mine.

My son, who does not share my inhibitions, could not resist your collective maternal magnetism. He could not escape the intoxication that your babies cast out with their tiny, flailing arms. He joined your blanket circle and took my shroud of invisibility with him. Suddenly your world and mine were one.

"I'm sorry," I said, and you looked up at me. "My son is invading your personal space," I explained.

"Oh, that's okay," you said cheerfully. I didn't know whether it really was okay or not. I decided to believe you and so he stayed at your side. You introduced yourself and asked, "What's your name?" just as you probably did when you were a child.

I told you my name, but I wished I was somebody else. I didn't know who else to be so I simply smiled.

You told me your children's names and ages. You were friendly, and in that moment the whole world seemed friendly. You were interested, though I had done nothing interesting. You told me about your mom's group, your community, and asked me if I lived nearby. You wrote down your number with a crayon and invited me to contact you.

And maybe someday, if I can find the right pair of shoes, I will.

The Mother at the Swings

by Vicki Forman

IT'S A SUNDAY AFTERNOON. My nine-year-old daughter, Josie, is at home drawing cartoons with my husband and I'm swinging my six-year-old son, Evan, at the park. Evan laughs and giggles and with each wide arc of the swing, his smile grows ever larger. The mother next to me smiles herself and says, "Boy, he really loves that, doesn't he? I mean, kids just love to swing, don't they?"

Yes, I think, *kids do love to swing*. But the reason my son loves to swing isn't the same reason her daughter, in the swing next to us, loves to swing. My son loves to swing because he is blind and nonverbal, because he has what is termed "sensory integration dysfunction" and requires enhanced "vestibular input." Swinging gives my son the kind of stimulation other kids, those who can see and talk and run and ride a bike, get by simply being and doing.

And, yes, he also loves to swing because all children love to swing.

I smile back at this mother and I swing Evan higher and he laughs louder, his squeals of delight growing bigger with every push.

"He really loves to go high," the mother at the swings says. "He's not afraid at all."

"He's not afraid because he can't see," I say. "He has no idea how high he's swinging."

"Well, he must have other ways of knowing," she says. "Because he definitely loves it."

My son was born at twenty-three weeks gestation, weighing only a pound. His twin sister died four days after birth when we removed her from life support. Evan was hospitalized for six months and came home blind, with feeding difficulties, chronic lung disease, and global developmental delays. Soon after that, he developed a serious seizure disorder and was on medication until his fourth birthday. He did not walk until he was five, still does not eat anything other than pureed baby food and formula from a cup, and has only a word or two—variations on "muh muh"—which he uses indiscriminately for "more" or "mama" or "open." I have watched my friends' newborns become toddlers and school-age children who can walk and laugh and talk and read, all while my son continues to function at the level of a two-year-old.

And yes, he has a beautiful laugh and a beautiful smile which grow only louder and wider on the swings.

When Evan was still in the hospital, a social worker gave us a handout, a road map for the potential reactions of friends and family members to our new status as parents of a super preemie. Potential support people came divided, according to the handouts, into the following categories: the rocks, the wanna-be-theres, and the gingerbread men. It warned us that people we might think were "rocks" could unexpectedly turn out to be "gingerbread men." *Just like in the story, they run, run as fast as they can from you when they hear of your baby's birth.*

I quickly found that the guide was right, that I was supported by only one or two rocks, and that the rest of my friends and family members had become gingerbread men. As Evan's disabilities became more obvious, after he left the hospital and in the time that followed, I found new rocks and said goodbye to the gingerbread men. And I found a new category for the characters in the social worker's handout: the mother at the swings.

The mother at the swings *wants to know*. It's why she makes her observations, and why she pretends there is nothing different, nothing dissimilar about her child and mine. *All kids love to swing.* The mother at the swings would like for me to tell her what it's like, how my son is different, and how he is the same. She wants to know about the cane he uses, and the challenges of having a nonverbal child, and how I manage to understand my son and communicate. She'd like to ask, *What does his future look like?* And *How are you with all this?*

She wants to know but she doesn't know how to ask. And so she tells me that all kids love to swing.

It has taken me years to know what to say to the mother at the swings, and how to say it. To reveal the truth, graciously. To let her in and help her understand. To tell her that yes, all children love to swing, and my son loves to swing and the reasons are both the same and different. That it's hard to watch her daughter, with her indelible eye contact and winning smile, and not mourn for what my son can't do. That some days my grief over my son is stronger than my love.

It has taken me even longer to appreciate the mother at the swings, to know that she and I have more in common than I once thought. To know that her curiosity is a mother's curiosity, one born out of love and tenderness and a desire to understand a child, my son, one who happens to be different. That she will listen and sympathize when I offer my observations. That her compassion and thoughtfulness mean she will take the knowledge I share and use it to understand other mothers like myself, some of whom could be her neighbor, her cousin, her sister, her friend. And, finally, that she wants to know so that she can teach her own child, who also loves to swing, how to embrace and treasure what makes us all different. And the same.

And the Shoes Will Take Us There in Spite of the Circumference

by Bobbi Lurie

Which world? I wonder as the therapist tells me my son
will never be able to live within it
Unless
Yes. I see the posed photos on her desk
(daughter? husband?) she points to the chart
which says my nine-year-old son is really five
She says my son's narrow interests (mathematics, Weird Al)
will not allow him to enter
the vast circumference of the universe
I stare into her double chin, down to the bunions on her feet
    pot belly, shirt tucked neat in her pants
She quotes Mel Levine who says *kids who are not well-rounded
            cannot succeed*
She sends me to a room where I pay $117 for the hour
A screaming infant reaches for her mother's glasses, throws
            them on the floor

Are you mad at me? my son asks as we walk out the door

I bend down, hold him so tight in my arms
So tight the green trees
So tight the blue and distant distant
Shape of my epiphany (were it half round, half yellow)
My son's small body, his heart pounds against my chest
   and this world
Of detritus and oblivious footnotes
How the fluid gold floats
How sound fills
Space and captures the tiniest beyond
Particles, waves,
Mass of sunlight wrapped around our legs
Our hands

To Persevere

by Ralph Savarese

YOU STOOD THERE FLAPPING, flapping at the crows,
uttering your customary whirring sound,
that moan I've come to think of as a prayer
whose words are incidental: stones the soul
might use to cross a stream—or not, the soul
being weightless. How hard it is at times
to lure you back to language and the peopled
world, so lost (or found) in light you seem.
This morning, working on a poem, I watched
you line up forks along the counter top.
My study seemed the prison you were making:
horizontal, bleak, the bar-like tines across
the page....I, too, was stuck. I called and called
my poem, but like a cat it wouldn't come;
I thought I heard it crawl beneath the house,
its ghost-like baby mews a sign of my
ineptitude or, worse, mere competence.
I tired of the words themselves. And so,
I nearly missed what you were flapping at:
that circus of the eye we learn to tame
with repetition of another sort.
Bird, we normals say. *Bird*, we write, and parse
the graphic aviary. No flapping here

but the dictionary's thousand paper wings,
each one clipped and paginated. (Yes,
your father like an ornithologist—
great morning *worder* he with wide-brimmed hat,
binoculars, and khaki cargo pants.)
Perception is a cage, glassed in, immense.
You flit about, find a vented opening;
move back and forth from "tree" to blazing tree.
The latter almost too particular—
the category fails; the leaves unleaf:
this vein, this stem, this curve, this green....**And yet,
at school** you hoard the highest grades, which stand
like soldiers for review, so plussed, so straight:
an honor guard the Generals thought (still think)
impossible. At ease, the sunlight says.
The anxious mind attends, the anxious heart
as well—as when you once announced, "Dad, freak
is ready for bed," the synthesizer's voice
too matter of fact, too monotone, for such
a sad reflection of our prejudice.
Your finger like a robin pecking at
the ground—spring's hopeful keys—but knowing better:
"There isn't room for me, not yet at least."
Mornings we wrestle on the double bed,
communicate with skull and skin—our cheeks
so close I lose the what of where. Pity
the eye accustomed to its throne. Pity
the word that does its monarch's bidding. Praise
the poet-father's necessary estrangement.
To see the world afresh! To *see* the world!
And then we're back to stubborn repetition:
doing laundry for the hundredth time,
laundry dried and folded, shirts so clean
a saint or pope could wear them—just to watch
the sudsy washer stage its revolution.
Just to mollify your nerves. O how

I've lost my cool, my hot, my lukewarm in
between. "Be reasonable!" I've shouted. "Get
out of the friggin' laundry room! You drive
me nuts!" And still you typed last Father's Day,
"I love you kind, great Dad. I really do."
This from a boy who cannot speak, a boy
the doctors claimed incapable of love
("no sense of self or others—he has no ToM"),
a boy who took *me* in at six, battered,
numb, having lost his mom and older sister.
What slack he cuts—and where it counts in life.
Accommodations for the testy parent!
An IEP! A PBS! You work
to get the best from me and I from you.
Perseveration's what they call this clenched
attachment to the ordinary—from
the verb "to persevere," as if persisting
steadily in something might reach a point
of aggravation for life's *obstacles*
(or other, less intense participants).
Does the world not wish to be observed?
Why precisely are we humans here?
"Autism sucks," you say, "but I see things
that you don't see." Perhaps such sight must come
with stereotypies, the neural networks
linked. "Behold!" the angels in the Bible
cry. Behold the strange, refulgent show—
this farm, this field, this sky, this cloud, this day—
acutest at its vanishing. When loss
resumes or **prejudice** excludes, when boredom
overtakes, I vow to persevere
with forks and crows and well-washed shirts. I want
my arms to flap and mouth to moan. I want
to feel your soul atop my stream-worn words.
You give the world your full and fierce regard.

The Visit

by Laura Shumaker

IT WAS 5:30 IN the morning, an hour before we needed to leave for the San Francisco Airport, but I was dressed and ready to go, and my husband, Peter, was rolling the luggage out to the car. My eighteen-year-old son, Matthew, who is autistic, had been home from Camphill Special School in Pennsylvania for spring break, and we were ready for him to leave.

"I like it better when Dad flies with me," said Matthew, who was polishing off his breakfast of three whole-wheat pancakes, perfectly stacked with a square of butter on top and maple syrup—just like the picture on the Aunt Jemima Buttery Lite label.

"I know," I said, shoving an Ativan bottle in my pocket for Matthew—just in case. "But it's my turn. We'll have fun."

Sending our first-born son to a residential school was the last thing Peter and I thought we would ever do. We had struggled through elementary and middle school with many ups and downs, most having to do with our son's impulsive behavior. Even as a toddler, Matthew had a knack for making people angry. He'd be sitting there with a dreamy look on his face one moment; the next he'd bolt across the room to bite someone, laughing all the way. We went through a number of "behaviorists" but Matthew outsmarted them all, and in recent years we'd weathered innumerable complaints from neighbors, visits from the police, and calls from school. Though exhausted and both showing physical signs of wear (scratches from Matthew, wrinkles from worry), we never considered "sending Matthew away"—until I pulled a letter from our mailbox that changed everything.

On letterhead from the law offices of McCracken, Doyle and Heatherby, it read:

"I am writing you regarding the bicycle accident involving your son, Matthew, on March 8, 2002 [about a month before] blah, blah, blah. . . ., I am representing so-and-so who was injured in the accident, please contact me, etc." I found Matthew, who was painting with watercolors in the kitchen. He looked so serene.

"Matthew," I had asked, "did you have an accident on your bike?"

"Who told you?"

"Someone wrote me a letter about it. Were you hurt?"

"Not really."

"Who else was in the accident?"

"A boy."

Oh, my God.

"Was he hurt?"

"Probably."

"Was he bleeding?"

"Pretty much."

God help me.

"Matthew," my voice quaking, "did an ambulance come?"

"I give up. I'm done talking about this."

It was clear that Matthew was no longer safe in the community where he had grown up, and his impulsive actions were putting others in peril. He needed more supervision, more than we or the local school could provide.

As one of the higher functioning students in his class at Camphill, Matthew was cast as the lead in the spring play, *Faust,* just before Spring Break. We thought it was far too ambitious for Matthew's teacher, Guy, to tackle such a challenging play, even when modified for the disabled students at Matthew's school. Peter and I and Matthew's two younger brothers sat anxiously in the front row, wondering how Matthew was going to pull off his debut, when the curtain opened. Matthew was the only character on stage, the professor sitting formally at his desk.

"Matthew would be good-looking if he weren't autistic," whispered my eleven-year-old son, John. It sounded unkind, but I knew what he meant. At eighteen, Matthew had grown into a handsome young man, with a tall, wiry frame, broad shoulders, and sandy blond hair. His expressive eyebrows frame his brown eyes, and his jaw is square and masculine.

But his exaggerated expressions and body carriage give him away. His forehead twists with intensity and he smiles too suddenly, with a wide goofy grin. There are moments when he appears composed, but then breaks into a hand-flapping, jumping-and-dipping flurry of activity—overstimulated by his environment and his mysterious internal world.

On the night of the play, however, Matthew was poised and fluid in his movements with composure we rarely see. He was an impressive Dr. Faust, and we were amazed at his command of his own, and everyone else's, lines. It was an emotional evening and there were tears of pride throughout the room.

With *Faust* behind us, our family looked ahead anxiously to the next couple of weeks with Matthew at home. (We always brace ourselves for these visits because even at their best, transitions make Matthew frantic.) Prior to one visit home, he made elaborate and detailed mental plans to hang out with his friends. The problem was, he had no friends. So he called students who had been kind to him five years ago during his first and only year in public high school.

His favorite was a girl named Jessica. He called her over and over. Her mother took most of the calls, and, I'm sure, wondered where in the heck I was. I eavesdropped on one conversation between Matthew and Jessica's mother in which Matthew was explaining that he was *so* lonely. "Why don't you call some of your friends?" she replied.

Our biggest worry about Matthew's visit this time was that his sixteen-year-old brother, Andy, had recently gotten his driver's license. While some people with autism have driver's licenses, it was clear to us that Matthew did not have the patience or the judgment to be one of them. Matthew knew it, too, and it bothered him—a lot. While aware of his disability, Matthew wanted desperately to be a regular guy like his brothers. He was infuriated that Andy, who was *two years younger*, might drive and he could not. To make matters worse, it seemed that every person he'd known since preschool was driving, even some of the special ed kids.

"Let's just tell him I failed my driving test," said Andy before Matthew's visit, "and I won't drive while he's home."

The first full day that Matthew was home was going well. Andy was in his room, talking to his girlfriend on the phone, and John was playing with a friend in the backyard. Matthew had just mowed the lawn and asked if he could wash my car. I thought this was fine and perhaps a good chore to distract him from lawn care, one of his current obsessions. He thoroughly washed the car and we praised him enthusiastically. He rewarded us with one of his wide, honest smiles.

He asked that since he had done such a great job, could he please drive the car five feet into the garage. His only experience with driving until then had been in the parking lot of our local church in Peter's car, with Peter's hand planted firmly on the emergency brake. We knew that this concession could further inspire Matthew to pursue getting a driver's license, but we were worn down by relentless petitioning.

In a moment of weakness, I asked Peter to sit in the passenger's seat of my car while Matthew drove the car into the garage. I stood in the driveway, and, already wondering what in the hell we were doing, watched Matthew get in the driver's seat. As Matthew started the car, Peter, who was not familiar with my car, asked, "Where is the emergency brake?"

Before I could reply, the car had plowed into the garage wall, crushing a number of full paint cans in its path and destroying two bicycles. Paint was everywhere, but fortunately, no one was hurt.

Andy, whose room shared a wall with the garage, ran out of the house looking dazed. "There's a big hole in my wall."

As we surveyed the damage in stunned silence, Matthew said that maybe he shouldn't drive until he was twenty-one. John offered to pay for the damage with his allowance money. Andy shook his head and resumed his telephone conversation with his girlfriend.

"I can't believe what idiots we are," Peter mumbled. We both recognized our lapse in judgment. We also knew that we had been driven to this by our desire to keep the peace and to try to help Matthew feel like a regular eighteen-year-old.

Matthew's remorse following the incident was genuine. We believed he would share our logic that this mishap proved that he should not drive the car this summer—or ever. Still, we hid all extra car keys and kept the ones we needed in our pockets.

In the days that followed, I kept Matthew very busy. He mowed and edged our lawn compulsively, so much that it looked like a putting green. I took him for a walk over the Golden Gate Bridge one day and then on a ferry boat ride to Alcatraz the next. We went bowling three days in a row, and I was beginning to crack. So I took him to the Blockbuster to rent video games, and we came home with a stack.

I must have set my keys down for a second while I got a diet Coke out of the fridge and popped it open.

Silence. Why was the house deadly quiet?

Where was Matthew?

"Matthew?" No answer. "MATTHEW?" I yelled out the back door. I walked out my front door and noticed the garage door was open. The car was gone.

BUT WHICH WAY?

The Middle School down the street—I'll bet he went there to show off.

I sprinted down the street in my clogs and around the corner to the middle school, my purse still hooked to my arm. Sure enough, there was my car parked crookedly in the parking lot, Matthew standing nearby looking scared, hugging his shoulders in reassurance, head down. A group of fourteen-year-old girls who had been playing basketball huddled nearby.

"He, like, almost totally hit us," said one. Another was crying to her mother on her cell phone.

Somehow, I got Matthew back in the car and drove him home. I knew it was important that I choose my words carefully. Keep it simple, I thought. Don't lose control.

Matthew sat across from me in our living room with a nervous smile, rocking and waiting. I was still out of breath from running, and from the horror of what could have transpired. Finally, I said, "I am very angry with you right now."

"Well, I'm angry with you for yelling at me in front of all those hot girls," he said, stomping his foot. "You should be proud of me for driving so well!"

And then as if on cue, the police car pulled into my driveway.

"Uh, oh," Matthew muttered.

With just a few more days until it was time to return Matthew to the safe and capable hands of his residential school, I thought back to the victorious scene at Camphill just a little over a week before when Matthew was taking a bow at the end of the play. I felt cheated. It just didn't seem fair that he did so well back in Pennsylvania but caused so much turmoil at home. Would we ever enjoy the fruits of his growth at school?

Matthew did not like to travel with me and he refused to sit with me.

"I don't see other eighteen-year-olds flying with their mothers," he said.

He liked to sit a few rows ahead of me when we flew, in a window seat. Once the plane took off, things almost always went well. On these trips I was anxious about who his seatmate would be, and how I could explain the situation without upsetting either the seatmate or Matthew.

Matthew liked to travel with his yearbook from his one year in regular high school. He used it as an icebreaker. When he saw someone at the airport that he wanted to talk to, he'd open his yearbook and display pictures of his "friends," his attempt to prove that he was a regular kid only further advertising his disability.

Going through Security was a problem, too, because Matthew wanted to appear as a regular guy traveling alone.

"Here, Matthew! Show the lady your ID!" I said cheerfully.

"*Don't look at me!*" he yelled, clutching his yearbook.

It didn't help that he was wearing brown socks with sandals and a Sponge Bob shirt, and that his fly was down.

"Pull up your zipper," I whispered.

"Go away!"

Everyone looked nervous. I quietly told the screener that Matthew was autistic, which I think she had already figured out.

"I'm not autistic," Matthew said as if there had been an egregious misunderstanding. "I'm a regular guy!"

Somehow we made it through, and I offered Matthew an Ativan, which he took with no dispute. When we got to the gate and began boarding the plane, Matthew glared at me and insisted, "I am not someone to be messed with!" I guessed that the Ativan hadn't kicked in yet.

We found our seats, and I tried to get a look at Matthew's seatmate. I avoided eye contact with my fellow passengers, whose anxious eyes were all on me, or so I felt, and I gave the flight attendant my speech.

"The young man in 18F is my son and he is autistic. He will be fine once he settles down. Please let the passenger next to him know, and I'm happy to answer any questions."

The flight attendant smiled at me compassionately, and I could feel my eyes filling up.

Right before takeoff, a round woman in her forties approached me. She had a short frumpy haircut and glasses. Her face was pleasant, but she looked nervous. She was Matthew's seatmate. She said she had heard about autistic people, but what should she do? What should she say? Is he brilliant like that guy in *Rain Man*?

I told her that he probably wouldn't talk much and would look out the window most of the time. I asked her to let me know if there was a problem.

Things did settle down once we were in the air. I spied on Matthew from time to time but could see only the top of his head. The flight attendant stopped by a few times and told me he was doing great. I casually glanced in his direction on the way to the bathroom, and his seatmate gave me thumbs up. I even dozed for a while, and everything seemed under control.

Matthew and I found each other after filing off the plane in Philadelphia. The plan was to meet his teacher, Guy, at the gate, and I would turn around and fly home. I usually rented a car and delivered Matthew to school myself and returned to California the next day, but I was needed at home by the rest of my family, who were still all reeling from the agitation of Matthew's visit.

As we looked for Guy, I heard running footsteps and a breathless voice calling "Matthew's mom! Matthew's mom!"

I turned around to find Matthew's seatmate with a big smile, looking exhilarated.

"Matthew was great!" she exclaimed. "He talked to me the whole time and showed me his yearbook. He wanted to know all the states I had been to. You have done such a great job with him. He is so nice! It wasn't at *all* what I expected!"

Guy appeared, and Matthew's face lit up. It was almost more than I could take. Once it was time to say goodbye, Matthew let me hug him, and then he pulled back and looked at me, still clutching his yearbook.

"Stop crying, Mom. Be happy." I watched Matthew and Guy walk away until they disappeared down the escalator toward baggage claim. I took a breath and called Peter.

"He's here. Flight went well. I'm boarding in forty-five minutes."

"It was a long break," Peter sighed, "you must be so relieved."

Relieved? Maybe. Strangely empty and lost was more like it.

It wasn't at all like I expected.

Is There Anything Else We Should Know?

by B. E. Pinkham

EARLY IN 2007, STATE of Illinois officials had to be convinced that our family was in danger as long as Stuart—my sweet, funny, fourteen-year-old autistic son—lived under our roof. In the blessed absence of police reports and emergency room records, what proof did I have? Our stories.

But after years as an empowered and optimistic parent with a reputation for maintaining a sense of humor, I resisted incarceration in this Opposite Land where all of our good stories were "bad" and all of our bad stories were "good." When our caseworker gently suggested that a particularly "good" story—meaning a truly frightening story—would have been more effective if I'd written it into the state's social history forms, and not left it for him to report through his notes, I told him, "I didn't get through the last ten years by dwelling on close calls, Jeff."

Not only had I not dwelled on that story, I hadn't even allowed it to enter my mind for months. Luckily, my husband remembered it and told Jeff at our last meeting. Those State officials needed to know precisely how Stuart's frequently destructive and aggressive behavior threatened our safety, sanity, and health or they would deny our request for funding for his residential care. They didn't need to know that his reading skills were approaching the second-grade level; they needed to know the fears that I'd never revealed to anyone.

During the previous year, I'd become terrified of doing things that were once routine for us. Stuart used to be happy and mostly cooperative on family field trips, but he'd begun having tantrums on the way into favorite places like the Field Museum. It took all of my strength just to shove him against a marble wall to prevent him crashing into toddlers or grandmothers. Sadly, it was time to admit that I could no longer keep innocent strangers safe, let alone my son or myself.

Therefore, my completed forms may have left out that one close call, but they included a three-page, single-spaced response to the final question:

Is there anything else you think we should know?

Yes. Small losses: bruises, bites, broken glass, square feet of plaster missing from the walls of every room, toys set on fire in the microwave. Oh—and Stuart so loved to hear his sister's guinea pig squeal that he unintentionally squeezed it to death. But is the Department of Human Services mandated to value domestic rodent life? Was that dramatic episode more or less convincing than our daily perils? His tantrums in the car that nearly caused accidents? My husband's severe hearing loss which endangered my son and daughter when I wasn't in the house?

Then there were secondary effects such as my eight-year-old daughter being too distractible to do her class work without a patient and watchful teacher. At home she barked and jumped like a puppy when a favorite adult arrived, hugged her school friends so tightly that she frightened them. And suddenly she couldn't sit through an animated movie in a theater. Were those symptoms of AD/HD or of the stress of living with her volatile 200-pound brother and the nervous, shrieking mother that came with the package? And, please don't think that I was boasting, but there was also my own medication-resistant depression/anxiety and the stress-related bowel disease that had put me in the hospital several times.

Is there anything else we should know?

Yes. After years of singing *Yes, I can!* filling out those forms became my debut as a diva of *No, I can't.* Of course, I'd written about my experiences with Stuart before then, but always post-crisis, in the glow of a victory. The hard truths were there, but those stories all ended on the upsweep with at least some optimism and a whiff of earned redemption. Now I had to renounce my faith in my ability to care for my child in order to get the services he needed—an experience another group home mother compared to a Christian being forced to deny Christ. And I did it. I *told* on him; I gave evidence against my son. The shame of that betrayal merged with the recognition of the truth in those stories to keep my head pounding and my stomach churning for five days.

Is there anything else we should know?

Yes. Of course I remember that day the previous summer on the beach at the end of our street. My husband and I swimming with our kids in Lake Michigan, and then warming ourselves on the sand. It seemed just a little bit reckless to sit there together with Eve and Stuart still out there, waist deep in the water. My husband, Arnell, disagreed. Maybe he's right, I thought, Stuart would never, even inadvertently, do anything to endanger his little sister. He adores her. But I stayed alert, watching Stuart's every move, watching my watchfulness, squinting through sunglasses as Arnell lay on his towel. We're like that: he's optimistic about the present moment—until something goes wrong—but pessimistic about our future. I always assume we'll all be okay in the lovely hazy future, but what *might* happen right here, right now, freaks me out.

I watched them splash, playing. Stuart laughing. Eve dolphin-leaping up and under. Both such strong swimmers. A plane razzed its single engine at us, turning there just below Chicago's northern border to circle south again with its cell phone banner ad in tow. Somebody kayaked past, beyond the buoys. Arnell wondered aloud if the radio-controlled airplane we'd seen the previous week might return. A jet ski howled away from the next beach south, zooming the kayak.

Then I saw Stuart's broad back, trouser cleavage, and red bathing suit as he dove under the water, but no Eve. The lifeguard on the concrete jetty had only two others to watch but she saw a game—nothing alarming. Eve's arm surfaced then vanished. I slapped my husband's leg and stood for a better view. Her open mouth appeared, her face sheeted in dark hair, but her brother's hand on her neck pulled her down.

"No! Stuart, stop!" The lifeguard looked at me, then him. They were both under again. Eve is less than half Stuart's size. He likes to pretend we can all swim underwater like the seals, penguins, and mermaids in his videos. He only wanted to watch her. He meant her no harm. I started running. Arnell passed me. I was not afraid for her life because we had plenty of time to save her—they were only thirty feet from the beach—plenty of time to wonder if I'd been stupid and callous.

Before Arnell's swimsuit was wet, Eve popped up ten feet away from her brother and kept going. I'd watched the beginning, the middle, the end, felt no surprise. We had plenty of time.

Eve walked out of the water, head down, round shouldered. She let me hug her with the towel. I told her she did the right thing, and she was a strong girl to swim away like that, and I was sorry. She nodded.

"He didn't mean to hurt you."

"I know, Mom." Everything I could say to her on the beach was already obvious, just the way it's always been for us.

"That was scary. You okay?"

She nodded. I thought of her dead guinea pig and everything I'd said then, and how forgiving she'd been as she cried, explaining to me that Stuart didn't understand what he did. This is what happens when her parents foolishly pretend to have a normal family.

While talking to Eve I'd heard Arnell say the inevitable phrase *bad behavior* to Stuart about six times. There was no guarantee he could understand *danger, drown,* or *death* in this context. *Hurt* didn't seem to cover it. Arnell sat Stuart on a towel and got to work stuffing goggles, towels, and water bottles into our beach bag. He dropped Tevas in front of Stuart.

"Put your sandals on. We're leaving." Stuart was smiling, impressed enough to sit still, but insulated from our mood.

That was Labor Day—our last beach day of the season anyway—and the fact that we could no longer let our kids swim together wouldn't be a problem until the lovely hazy future of the next summer. We walked home. I allowed myself to put the episode out of my mind for the winter.

Is there anything else we should know?

Yes. No matter how true those stories, no matter how many dear friends and respected professionals enthusiastically assured me that I was doing the right thing at the right time, no matter what I knew intellectually about the benefits to Stuart of a more structured daily routine, placing my son in a group home felt like complete failure, like giving up.

That's why I sobbed in his new room on the Monday that he moved in. After dropping him off at school that morning, I'd gone to the group home to make his bed with the blue sheets and blanket bought to replicate his bed at our home. I needed to borrow a roll of toilet paper from the bathroom to dab and blow while arranging his clothes in the tall oak dresser—a spare that we'd brought from his room. I taped a poster of the solar system to the wall over his new bed. The agency that runs his school runs the house in cooperation with the parents. They take care of our kids; we do as much as we can for them, including clothing our children and setting up their rooms. My son, they told me, would now have two homes: one with us and one with his school friends. He could call them Mom and Dad's House and the Kids' House. I fought my guilt, trying to see it as an addition to his world, not a subtraction. But when one staff member called this the day that Stuart would *permanently* move in with them, the word sank through me like a stone.

Stuart had visited the house twice before his move-in day: the first time with me. The second time had been just the night before, for dinner with his five new housemates and the staff. After leaving him there, Arnell and I took ourselves to one of Oak Park's most popular restaurants, but we lacked the spirit to match the roof deck's festive lights and umbrellas. We smiled at the waiter while ordering sensible salads and chicken sandwiches. I drank a margarita and wished it were a lot stronger but knew better than to order a second. All around us, well-groomed parents fed toddlers in highchairs, cut meat for little girls in party dresses. I felt like a wizened mortal among naïve deities—but it was hardly my first time feeling that.

Arnell and I tried to talk about Stuart. Perched on a sharp ridge between loss and hope, the future and the past were both obscured. We talked about Eve instead, expecting that she'd worked through her homesickness by then—she was away at her first sleepover camp. By the time her camp would be over in six days, Stuart would be home with us again for the weekend.

We finished the meal too quickly, leaving ourselves with an hour to kill before picking Stuart up after his dinner at the house. We zig-zagged in our car like Pac Man through the residential grid until we stumbled upon the Frank Lloyd Wright Home and Studio. Why not stop for a stroll? Contemplating the plaque and dark geometry of that house from the sidewalk with the other tourists, I realized that almost exactly ten years ago, on June 28th, 1997, we'd all been there—even Eve, in the form of her DNA. We didn't know yet, but she'd been conceived the evening before. Arnell and Stuart had driven me to the Wright Home and Studio for a tour with my design school class. Just three months before then, in March of '97, we'd sat in the comfort of our own bedroom and diagnosed our four-year-old's autism using a rating scale sent home in his preschool backpack.

But on that evening in 2007, I wasn't ready to sort through an avalanche of years. We headed back to the car holding hands, saying almost nothing. I counted on the centrifugal pull of our velocity and change of direction to carry us through the week.

Is there anything else we should know?

Yes. Dropping him off at school the next morning, I attempted a breezy goodbye and held off the tears until I got back in the car. He would arrive by school bus with the rest of his new housemates that afternoon, after I'd prepared his room and left.

His school principal—one of his favorite people—rearranged her schedule to greet him at the group home on his move-in day. Because he was anxious and quietly frightened, she stayed into the evening. They were sitting close together on the sofa watching one of his favor-ite videos about animals, when he said, "Paula's suitcase. Pajamas on."

She knew, as I would have, that he meant: *You're staying here with me tonight, right? Your suitcase is here somewhere, right? Please put on your pajamas so that I can stop worrying that you're going to leave me.*

After making sure that Stuart would not be too anxious to sleep, Paula went to her home. If I'd been there, he would have been at least confused and probably in a panic to leave with me. Meanwhile, Arnell and I were in our suddenly childless house, attempting to watch a favorite old movie for comfort, without any hope of enjoying it. We were grateful that Paula's bond with Stuart could bridge the gap between our home and his new one.

Then, within days, the house staff reported that they were enjoying Stuart's sense of humor—a huge relief to me since it meant he felt safe enough to relax with them and allow them into his world.

Is there anything else we should know?

Yes. Over the next weeks and months Stuart seemed to adjust to the new routines more easily than I did. At first, the end of our weekends with him would reveal my guilt and anxiety. I fretted over his supply of clothes and medications for the week, worried that our perfectly reliable car might break down on the fifty-minute drive to his Kids' House. But Stuart quickly figured out it was best to just ignore me and help his dad pack his toys and DVDs and get in the car.

We have always held him close. We have always kept him moving. We haven't done absolutely everything we could have for him, but I regret very few decisions and I've forgiven myself for most of the rest. I've learned that doing the right thing can still leave parents feeling wrong and resigned. When other parents like us claim that the lows have been matched by the highs, I feel sure that they are delusional, but maybe they are better off that way.

In some ways, Stuart's departure from his parents' house was a natural progression—and certainly we were extremely lucky that the option was available when we needed it. But I still feel some guilt over the luxurious peace of our home when he is not in it.

After her brother had been in the group home for a year, without anyone reminding her, Eve mentioned the time that Stuart tried to drown her (her words) as proof that she understood why he needed to live there. As I write this, she is ten. She still sometimes has more energy than she can control, but I'm able to structure activities around her needs for the first time in her life.

And my son is learning to take care of himself and to do his own laundry at the Kids' House. He spends at least every other weekend at Mom and Dad's House where we let him rule the DVD player and eat too much. We're taking field trips to his favorite museums again. When we bring him back to his house on Sunday evenings, he hangs his coat and backpack on his hook and carries his duffel bag full of dinosaur and Transformer toys up to his room. After I've checked through his dresser drawers and talked to the staff for a few minutes, he asks me to leave by saying, "Penguin kiss." He leans down to present his cheek to me. Everyone in our family has their own personalized good-bye and hello rituals based on scenes in his videos. Arnell is the t-rex. Eve is the bear cub. I'm the penguin, and if I don't waggle my head like a penguin properly and make the right kinds of squeaks as I kiss Stuart, we have to start over. He's very patient with me.

Is there anything else we should know?

Yes. We're telling good stories again, like the one about our visit to an amusement park this past summer. He wanted to fly through corkscrews and be flung upside down by roller coasters that would completely unnerve his sister and father. So I gladly resigned myself to enjoying the thrills with him. Stuart waited patiently with all the other teenagers for his turn to ride the wildest coasters named Superman, Batman, and the Demon. At the top of the last big one I screamed, "This is what I do for love!" into the spinning blue sky.

We're all calmer, safer, and healthier. No one has failed and no one has given up.

The Family Gangsta

by James Wilson

MY SON SAM AND I have reached a standoff of sorts, an uneasy accommodation. I understand him, more or less; and he understands me, more or less. We spend far too much time together, and because of that we sometimes get tired of each other. As often as I complain about the difficulty of being the primary companion of an autistic 26-year-old, he complains about the difficulty—and boredom—of having to put up with a 58-year-old assistant. "I'm tired of you," he'll say. "You're too old for me."

Call it a hard-fought truce.

Still, I'm a realist. I've spent too much time on the psych ward to fool myself into thinking that the bad old times won't come again. Autism can't be cured or outgrown. Just last year Sam could be quietly reading the phonebook one moment and then BAM, I look up and he's banging his head against the wall. Sometimes not even listening to music or watching the weather channel would calm his turbulent mind. The forecast might remain unchanged from one 15-minute segment to the next, but not Sam. Some subtle, imperceptible change in intonation or camera angle would set off a chain reaction. Serotonin would surge, dopamine receptors would tweak, and suddenly all hell would break loose. Without warning, Sam would rush through the house smashing and head-banging everything in range, looking for...me? Yikes!

Let me be blunt. I've found that when all else fails and heads start banging, only dark humor can help me cope. I've earned my right to be sardonic. I've been punched, kicked, scratched, and bit. I've been pushed down stairs and shoved into walls. One day I suffered the indignity of being chased around my front yard by my broom-wielding son in full view of our neighbors. Hahaha, just Sam having a bad moment. Not to worry, really. He'll calm down in a second.

No question, Sam can be difficult. Yet, on other occasions he can be absolutely delightful, a pleasure to have as a life companion. At 5'8" he's a stocky 190 pounds with a more or less neatly trimmed beard and curly brown hair tucked under a baseball cap. In addition to autism, Sam has a mood disorder. When he's down, he'll sit slumped forward with his head listing to the right and his eyes half closed as though he were hibernating. But when he's wired, he paces around the house either humming or buzzing like a bee and tapping on walls and tables. For the past several years he's lived semi-independently in a fully equipped apartment in our basement dubbed the "Yellow Submarine" after its sunny yellow paint and a poster of the Beatles's movie of the same name hanging on the wall. His three other companions, all males, spend time in Sam's bachelor pad and take him out to movies and restaurants.

Unlike many people on the autism spectrum, Sam chatters nonstop about his favorite topics. His current obsessions are severe weather, especially tornadoes, and rap music, courtesy of his youngest companion, who introduced Sam to the likes of Jay-Z, Snoop Dogg, Busta Rhymes, Outkast, Dr. Dre, Ludacris, 50 Cent, Jurassic 5, and the ever-popular NWA. Sam and rap are a perfect fit. He loves the word play and the repetitive, pounding rhythms. Thanks to his friend, appropriately nicknamed Party Dawg, Sam has gone gangsta.

Now Sam comes hip-hopping down the hallway singing along with his headphones: "Drop it like it's hot! Drop it like it's hot!" Or "Bust a move! Bust a move!"

Sam walks the walk and talks therRap. "Wassup?" he'll ask, when he hasn't seen me for all of five minutes. Or he'll tell me he's feeling "all eaten up" when he's not quite himself. "Hook me up," he'll say, when he wants something, usually food. He introduces his friends as his "homies." Sometimes he'll go back and forth between rap talk and weather talk, as though he's engaging in parallel conversations. Just what the world needs: a playa with an obsessive-compulsive interest in meteorology.

Sam doesn't work; he has never been able to hold down a job, partly because of the kinds of jobs people have offered him. Once in high school he was told by a job counselor to break down boxes since that was all someone with "reduced potential" could possibly do. Then after high school he was sent to a sheltered workshop and told to put screws in a box for 24 cents an hour. It would be hard to imagine a task less suited for a person who has problems with concentration, sensory overload, and fine motor coordination but who has above average intelligence. Not surprisingly, Sam refused to cooperate with his job counselors, acted up, and got sent to the showers.

So instead of working, Sam recreates. But enough telling, let me show you Sam in action. Recently, Sam's social club, which caters to young adults with various disabilities, sponsored a special outing, a first ever Boy's Night Out. Where does our fearless outing leader, Tim, decide to take us? To Hooters, of course. And not just any Hooters, but the fancy marina-style Hooters on the Ohio River in downtown Cincinnati.

Everyone arrives early, ready to party. Together, we're a rainbow of ages, ethnicities, and disabilities. Sam and the other members of his club walk across the wooden ramp one at a time, accompanied by a couple of the fathers who serve as helpers, myself included. We don't have to worry about fitting in at Hooters. We're not the weirdest dudes here. None of the other customers even notices us. Not the group of Japanese businessmen, not the two grungers wearing heavy metal T-shirts, not the single guy pretending to be reading a newspaper, and certainly not the old geezers sitting at the bar nursing their beers. They're much too busy ogling the Hooters girls to care about a few extraordinary young men limping and shuffling across the wooden floor. The server girls are wearing their standard-issue tight shorts and tighter orange tops. The classy look.

"Man—this beats last month's outing," says one of our troops when he spots his first Hooter's babe.

"I take care of my guys," says Tim, our fearless leader, a stocky young man with shoulder-length brown hair. Tim plays in a rock band and appears absolutely unflappable. Nothing ruffles Tim's feathers as he supervises his group: John jumping up and down at the table, Eric scribbling in his notebook left to right, then top to bottom, and Sam asking repeatedly about tornadoes. Just another night for City Club, a social club for young people with disabilities sponsored by the United Way. Our version of "normal." Whatever normal means.

Unable to attain Tim's Zen-like state of unflappability, I keep worrying that one of our charges will reach out and grab a handful of Hooters flesh. My bad. Ironically, our guys are less distracted by Hooters babes than the other customers are. Mostly, we want spicy chicken wings, platters of fries, and a round of drinks, thank you very much. Sure, we enjoy the sexy costumes, but the girls represent only one item on our party platter and definitely not the main course. We're here to party, not to ogle. We don't get out all that much. As you can probably guess, our social calendars aren't very full. But when we do go out on the town, watch out. Let the good times roll!

And for not ogling, the Hooters girls love us. Sure, we're a little strange, but at least we're not sexist pigs. No boorish behavior coming from our table. Just John, the youngest of our group, who is largely nonverbal, bouncing in his seat saying "Hi!" over and over again. So the girls hover around us two and three at a time, like a burst of orange butterflies fluttering around our flowers. They can't resist our charm. And who can blame them? How often does a group of young, distinctive, well-behaved gentlemen appear among Hooters's usual clientele?

We're about to order when Eric, a young man about Sam's age, turns to his server and asks, "Do you have a death ray in your mind?"

Hahaha, everyone laughs. Good one, Eric. Our server, a blonde bombshell, blushes ever so slightly. She's been asked worse, no doubt. "No, I don't," she says playfully. "But I can take your order if you're ready."

Eric likes that. You bet. Everyone tries to order at the same time until our server has to raise her hand high, like an umpire calling time out. "One at a time, boys."

When it's Sam's turn, he asks, "Which do you like better, rap or hip hop?"

"Oh," she says. "I'm not sure I know the difference?"

Sam's already on to the next topic. "Have you ever seen a tornado? Do you remember the Blue Ash tornado on April 9, 1999? Have the sirens ever gone off here?"

"Whoa," our server says. "You must like weather."

"And fire alarms," Sam adds. He reaches out and touches her bare arm lightly, then thinks twice about it and snaps his hand back. "Sorry," he says, and means it.

Sam turns to me. "Was I appropriate?" He tends to worry about his behavior—after the fact.

"Well...you shouldn't touch, but . . ." I don't know how to finish my sentence.

"It's okay," our server says, all smiles.

When Sam orders, he always begins with the same question: "Which do you have, Coke or Pepsi?" Not that it matters, since whichever they have is what he orders. But Sam has to follow his ritual. His next question is: "Do you have pizza or chicken tenders?" Pizza and chicken tenders represent the staff of life for Sam. Only on rare occasions will he break his routine and order a cheeseburger, as long as the server understands that no lettuce, tomato, onion, or pickle should touch his cheeseburger. If vegetable touches burger, we're in for a bumpy ride.

"We have chicken tenders, served with lots of French fries," our server responds.

"Yeah, baby. Pile it on!"

Everybody agrees. Pile it on!

When the food comes, we pounce. We might not be pretty to watch, with stacks of extra napkins and wet wipes all around, but no one could ever accuse us of not enjoying our food.

Later, when we've pretty much finished eating, most of us bearing the telltale signs of catsup and barbecue sauce, the servers take turns coming over to visit. We've won them over with our good looks, charming behavior, and healthy appetites.

Then Andrew, our oldest, jumps up and heads for the gift counter. Someone jokes that he wants to buy a Hooters outfit for his mom.

Yeah, right, wouldn't she love that? But when he returns, it's with a Hooters T-shirt for himself. We all agree that Andrew will be one handsome dude in his new Hooters T-shirt. Always a ham, Andrew pulls the T-shirt over his head, eyeglasses and all, just so we can see how good he looks. He straightens his glasses and mugs for us and the ladies. Joking, one of the servers asks if he wants to work at Hooters.

Meanwhile, Sam has cornered another server. "What about the Xenia tornado of 1974? That's famous, you know. The biggest outbreak of tornadoes in recorded history."

"Really…"

"Yeah, I have a book on that one. Do you like fire alarms?"

"No, I don't like alarms. They're too loud."

"Me neither. Except for Simplex. Do you have any Simplex fire alarms here?" When she doesn't answer, Sam says, "That's okay, not everybody has a Simplex."

When we leave, it's with a sense of satisfaction, with the knowledge that we made new friends and interacted with everyone, including the Hooters girls, and that we partied to the max and left quite an impression. We have the T-shirts and catsup stains to prove it. Someone wants to know when and where Tim's rock band will be playing, so that we can continue the party, whenever. Let's do Hooters again. Why not? Hooters rules!

Sam and I are the last to leave. He's made it this far without a serious gaffe. But suddenly he reaches out and takes our server's hand and looks deeply into her eyes. "If you were president, you'd be Babe-raham Lincoln," he says, repeating a line from the movie *Wayne's World*.

She laughs. "Thank you—I think!"

I breathe a sigh of relief. He could have repeated his favorite line from *Austin Powers: Goldmember*. The one about shagging!

"Did I blow my cover?" he asks on the way out the door, a big grin on his face.

I have to laugh. "No, we did well."

At that Sam says, "Bust a move!" and does a hip-hop dance shuffle on the deck. Then he heads for the ramp that will take him to shore, with me following along behind.

Contributors

Anonymous's son is doing beautifully in a mainstream school. She's met many wonderful teachers and therapists because of him.

Cheri Brackett is a Psychotherapist and certified Spiritual Director who lives in Asheville, NC, with her husband, Tom, and daughter, Audrey. She delights in journeying with individuals and families who find themselves in places of "otherness" in their lives. She is also a speaker, painter, and freelance writer. Cheri can be reached at cabrackett@bellsouth.net.

Grey Brown is the author of *When They Tell Me* from Finishing Line Press, 2009, and *Staying In*, winner of the North Carolina Writers' Network Chapbook contest. Her poems have appeared in the *Violet, The Greensboro Review, Iris, The West Coast Poetry Journal, Mothering Magazine, Cold Mountain Review, Wilmington Review, Blue Pitcher, Paris Atlantic,* and others. Grey is the director of the literary arts program for Health Arts Network at Duke Medical Center. She is currently working on her first full length collection of poems, to be released by Turning Point Press in 2010. Her website is at www.greybrownpoetry.com.

Kristina Chew is an Associate Professor of Classics at Saint Peter's College in Jersey City, New Jersey. She is writing a book (working title: *We Go with Him*) about autism, language, and translation; has published a number of articles about literature about autism, disabilities studies, and literature; and has made numerous presentations about advocacy, teaching college students who have ASDs, and literature about autism. From 2006-2009 she wrote two widely-read blogs about autism, Autism Vox and the autism blog at Change.org; she now writes daily about life with Charlie on the road in Autismland at kristinachew.com. She has also published a translation of Virgil's *Georgics* (2002) and written about classics and multiculturalism. Her son, Charlie, was born in 1997.

Barbara Crooker's book, *Radiance*, won the 2005 Word Press First Book Award, and was a finalist for the 2006 Paterson Poetry Prize. Her second book, *Line Dance* (Word Press, 2008), won the 2009 Paterson Prize for Literary Excellence. Her third book, *More,* will be published in 2009 by C & R Press. Her poems appear in a variety of literary journals and many anthologies, including *Good Poems for Hard Times* (Garrison Keillor, editor)(Viking Penguin). She has won a number of awards, including the WB Yeats Society of NY Prize (Grace Schulman, judge), the Thomas Merton Poetry of the Sacred Prize (Stanley Kunitz, judge), and the *Rosebud* Ekphrastic Poetry Award. She is the mother of a twenty-five-year-old son with autism.

Ann Douglas is the creator of the internationally bestselling *The Mother of All® Books* series and *The Mother of All Solutions*, the co-author of *The Unofficial Guide to Having a Baby and Trying Again: A Guide to Pregnancy After Miscarriage, Stillbirth, and Infant Loss*, and, along with her daughters, wrote the award-winning body image book for teens, *Body Talk: The Straight Goods on Fitness, Nutrition, and Feeling Great about Yourself.* She contributes to numerous pregnancy and parenting magazine in addition to her own columns in *Yahoo! Canada*, and *Conceive Magazine*. Ann is the mother of four children, ages 10 through 20, including Ian, who has Asperger's syndrome. She lives with her family in Canada.

Drama Mama is an actor, teacher, and mother of two small girls, one on the autism spectrum, one not. She writes about her life on her blog, http://likeashark.blogspot.com.

Kimberly K. Farrar is a writer and teacher currently living in Astoria, New York. She has a B.A. in Creative Writing from the University of Arizona, and an M.A. in TESOL from Hunter College. She teaches in her community. Her work has been published in *Long Shot, Lullwater Review, Mudfish, The Ledge, Voices of Autism,* and other literary journals.

Veronika Hill is a former software programmer who is finding her passion as a writer and mother. She has one son, nicknamed Taz, who is extremely active and alert. He keeps her busy from the wee hours of the morning until lights-out at night. When she's not following him around town, she can often be found Googling her special interests obsessively. You can read about those and more at veronikahill.com.

Following a career in modern dance, **Maggie Kast** received an M.F.A. in fiction from Vermont College. She has published fiction in *The Sun, Nimrod, Rosebud, Paper Street, Kaleidoscope,* and others, and essays in *Image: Art, Faith, Mystery, Writer's Chronicle,* and others. She is currently working on a memoir, excerpts of which have appeared in *ACM* (*Another Chicago Magazine*) and *America,* and she teaches writing at Columbia College Chicago.

Janet Kay works as a creative director and writer in St. Louis, Missouri. She is at work on her first novel.

Anjie Kokan is a member of the Wisconsin Fellowship of Poets and The Wasteland Poets. Her work has appeared in *Mamazine, Free Verse, Bellowing Ark,* and *Chrysanthemum.*

Susan T. Layug's personal essays have won awards both in the United States and her native land, the Philippines. Some of her work has been produced and read on Chicago Public Radio. Her poetry has also appeared online and in print, the most recent of which is in *Field of Mirrors: An Anthology of Philippine American Writers.*

Bobbi Lurie's collections of poetry, *The Book I Never Read* and *Letter from the Lawn,* were published by CustomWords. "And the Shoes Will Take Us There In Spite of the Circumference" was previously published in *Wild Plum.*

Mama Mara worked as an editor and speechwriter until 1996, when she answered her true calling by becoming an autism treatment specialist, educational paraprofessional, insurance rights advocate, speech therapist, pharmaceutical expert, and mental health "counselor" (in other words, a special-needs mother). She lives in Wisconsin with her two boys, Rocky and Taz, who absolutely make her life worthwhile.

Bruce Mills teaches literature at Kalamazoo College. In his field, he has authored two books, including, most recently, *Poe, Fuller, and the Mesmeric Arts: Transition States in the American Renaissance* (2005). In the last few years, he has turned to creative nonfiction, which has been published in *The Georgia Review* and *New England Review.* His essay "Flood Plain" is part of a recently completed memoir entitled *An Archaeology of Yearning*, a book that explores memory, story, and desire in a home transformed by autism. In addition to teaching, Bruce has also been active in his local autism society and presently serves as a board member on The Gray Center for Social Learning and Understanding. He lives in Kalamazoo, Michigan, with his wife, Mary Holtapp, daughter Sarah, and son Jacob.

Mary McLaughlin has carved out a space in small-town New Hampshire, where she works in student affairs and teaches writing at Colby-Sawyer College, and in the blogosphere, where she writes as Mom—Not Otherwise Specified at http://momnos.blogspot. com. Both her blog and her life revolve around her son.

MothersVox blogs at *Autism's Edges* (www.autismsedges.blogspot. com). She lives in New York City with her husband and daughter.

Aileen Murphy is the author of a chapbook, *There Will Be Cats* (Finishing Line Press), and the Assistant Director of Creative Writing at

Virginia Tech, where she has taught writing since 1994. She is also the Co-Director of the Southwest Virginia Writing Project. She lives with her husband, Paul, and her two children in Blacksburg, Virginia.

During the 1980s, **B. E. Pinkham** was an artist and earned all the fine art degrees she would ever want. During the 1990s, she was a landlord and acquired all the buildings and tenants that she would ever want. By 2000, she was a mother and had all the children she would ever want. Since then, she's been writing. She hasn't yet written everything she wants. Her work has appeared in *Brain, Child Magazine.* She is seeking a publisher for her memoir, *Let Me Look at You,* in which autism plays a shockingly minor role.

Lesley Quinn is an essayist and writing coach who specializes in assisting high school seniors create deeply felt and compelling college application essays. Her work has been published in *The New York Times, The San Francisco Chronicle,* and numerous literary magazines and anthologies. She lives with her husband, a psychologist, and her daughter when she's visiting, in Berkeley, California.

Ralph James Savarese is the author of *Reasonable People: A Memoir of Autism and Adoption,* which *Newsweek* called a "real life love story and a passionate manifesto for the rights of people with neurological disabilities." His poems, essays, translations, criticism, and opinion pieces have appeared, among other places, in *American Poetry Review, Sewanee Review, New England Review, Southwest Review, Modern Poetry in Translation, The Journal of Literary and Cultural Disability, Leviathan: A Journal of Melville Studies, The New York Times, The LA Times, The Houston Chronicle, The Atlanta Journal Constitution,* and *The Des Moines Register.* In January 2010, he will publish, with his wife, a co-edited issue of *Disability Studies Quarterly* devoted to the topic of "Autism and the Concept of Neurodiversity."

Susan Segal is the author of *Aria,* a novel, and numerous award-winning short stories. She is assistant professor of creative writing at the University of Southern California and an editor at *Coast Magazine* in

Orange County, CA, where she lives with her son. She is at work on a collection of short stories.

Laura Shumaker is the author of *A Regular Guy: Growing Up with Autism,* a memoir about raising her autistic son, Matthew, to young adulthood. She is a regular contributor to NPR Perspectives and a columnist for www.5minutesforspecialneeds.com. Laura's essays have appeared in the *San Francisco Chronicle*, the *Contra Costa Times*, the *East Bay Monthly*, *The Autism Advocate,* on *cnn.com*, *A Cup of Comfort,* and *Voices of Autism* among others. Laura speaks regularly to schools and book and disability groups and lives in Lafayette, California with her husband, Peter, and her three sons.

Chantal Sicile-Kira is an autism advocate, international speaker, parent, and award-winning author known for providing hope and practical strategies to both families and educators. Chantal's first book, *Autism Spectrum Disorders*, was the recipient of the 2005 Autism Society of America's Outstanding Literary Work of the Year Award. Her books, *Adolescents on the Autism Spectrum* and *Autism Life Skills*, are also published by Penguin. Chantal is a blogger on the Huffington Post, moderates webinars for momsfightingautism.com, and occasionally hosts radio shows on Autism One Radio. Her family was highlighted in *Newsweek* and on MTV's documentary series True Life "I Have Autism," which was the recipient of a 2008 Voice Award. For more information visit www.chantalsicile-kira.com.

Kristen Spina is a freelance writer living in New York whose writing has appeared in numerous trade and consumer publications. She is currently at work on a novel, and you can read more of her writing at http://kristenspina.wordpress.com.

Christine Stephan, a program certified RDI® consultant, lives in Virginia with her husband and three sons. She and her family can often be found navigating the streets of her hometown by bicycle. Christine writes about her family, autism, and RDI on her blog, DaySixtySeven: http://www.daysixtyseven.blogspot.com.

Carolyn Walker is an essayist, memoirist, poet, journalist, and teacher. Her work has appeared in *Hunger Mountain, The Southern Review, Crazyhorse, Columbia: A Journal of Literature and Art, The Writer's Chronicle,* and *Encore.* She has authored a memoir about the life of her developmentally disabled daughter, called *Every Least Sparrow.* A graduate of the Vermont College Master of Fine Arts in Writing program, she is married and the mother of three children. She lives in Michigan.

Emily Willingham is a biologist and freelance writer and editor. She lives in Austin, Texas, with her soul mate and spouse, Marshall, and their three sons, Tom Henry, Will, and George. Her published work includes the upcoming *Complete Idiot's Guide to College Biology* and pieces in *Backpacker* and other national, regional, and local publications.

In addition to being the primary companion of his now 28-year-old autistic son, **James C. Wilson** is a professor of English and journalism at the University of Cincinnati. He has published five books, including *Weather Reports from the Autism Front: A Father's Memoir of His Autistic Son (2008).*

Editors

Kyra Anderson chronicles life as a homeschooling mom and writer on her blog, thismom. com. Her work has appeared in *Tiny Lights, Bust Out,* and *100 Hats,* among other small presses. Her memoir, *How My Son's Asperger's Saved My Ass,* is not yet published. She lives in New England with her son and children's book writer/illustrator husband, David Milgrim.

Vicki Forman is the author of *This Lovely Life: A Memoir of Premature Motherhood.* Her work has appeared in the *Seneca Review* and the *Santa Monica Review* as well as the anthologies, *Love You to Pieces: Creative Writers on Raising a Child with Special Needs, This Day: Diaries from American Women,* and *Literary Mama: Reading for the Maternally Inclined.* She lives outside Los Angeles with her husband and daughter.